CRAIG S. KEENER

For All Peoples:

*A Biblical Theology
of Missions in the
Gospels and Acts*

Foreword by Wonsuk Ma

Book 2 of the APTS Press Occasional Papers Series

WIPF & STOCK · Eugene, Oregon

Wipf and Stock Publishers
199 W 8th Ave, Suite 3
Eugene, OR 97401

For All Peoples
A Biblical Theology of Missions in the Gospels and Acts
By Keener, Craig S. and Ma, Wonsuk
Copyright © 2020 APTS Press All rights reserved.
Softcover ISBN-13: 978-1-7252-8612-2
Hardcover ISBN-13: 978-1-7252-8611-5
eBook ISBN-13: 978-1-7252-8613-9
Publication date 8/17/2020
Previously published by APTS, 2020

TABLE OF CONTENTS

Publisher's Preface
to the Occasional Papers Series

This book is the second in the *APTS Press Occasional Papers Series*. The first book, *Pentecostals and the Poor: Reflections From the Indian Context*, by Ivan Satyavrata, is available through our website, www.aptspress.org.

The purpose of this series to produce smaller books comprised of articles that deal with theological, anthropological and missiological issues relevant to serving God in Asia. From time to time, other sciences may also be so employed. As the title suggests, the books will be published as articles of interest to our readers become available.

For further information on this series or other work of the APTS Press, including our journal, the *Asian Journal of Pentecostal Studies*, please contact us through the website.

Sincerely,

Dave Johnson, DMiss
Series Editor

FOREWORD

Today, Christian missions is in the blessed state of utter confusion!
The claim "evangelization of the world in our generation"
represented the "holy confidence" of the Edinburgh Missionary
Conference (1910) among the western mission leaders. This
"confidence" may have been confused with the western political or
colonial power. Ironically, as the colonial system broke down, global
Christianity shifted radically and grew exponentially. With almost
two-thirds of world Christians now living in the three southern
continents, and their immigrant communities bringing new energy to
the waning churches in the North, a large space has opened up for
creative rethinking of Christian witnessing. Hence, the rethinking and
revisioning process of mission urges us all to go back to the Scripture
afresh, devoid of any cultural lenses but listening to the Holy Spirit.

Given this unique locus of today's church, this book takes us back
to the foundational teachings of Jesus on missions: the Great
Commission (Gospel of Matthew) and the Messianic Commission
(Gospel of John). Although these two passages are "universal" in
grounding Christian mission, Professor Keener wants to assure that the
role of the Holy Spirit is central to Christian living and acting as God's
witnesses. The chapter on Pentecost is an important contribution not
only to Pentecostals in missions but the entire Christian church. The
growth of Pentecostal Christianity, which has fueled the radical shift
in and expansion of the global church, will find that this chapter serves
as the firm foundation for Spirit-empowered witnessing. The last
chapter presents the fundamental and equally challenging feature of
global missions: crossing barriers. This drive to embrace diversity and
desire for unity appears counter-intuitive and even counter–norm. This

seeming contradiction can take place only when Christ's followers invite the work of the Holy Spirit into their life! At the end of this rather short reading, one is left with a deep sense that we have been commissioned to live, work, and proclaim in this world as Christ's witnesses through the power of the Holy Spirit. Implicitly, the book also urges the readers to redefine missions in the Spirit!

Wonsuk Ma, PhD
Dean, Distinguished Professor of Global Christianity
College of Theology and Ministry, Oral Roberts University

ENDORSEMENTS

Craig Keener, one of the finest and most prolific NT scholars of our day, has produced another gem. *For All Peoples: A Biblical Theology of Missions in the Gospels and Acts* blends together rich scholarly insights, rooted in an unsurpassed knowledge of the first-century world, with an edifying and pastoral eye that is always focused on the radical nature of Jesus' call to follow him in his redemptive mission. Successive chapters illuminate the seminal contributions that Matthew, Luke, John, and Paul make to a biblical theology of missions. The final chapter, rooted in the narrative of Acts, appropriately ties together these themes by describing Paul's Macedonian vision as a call for the Church to take the gospel from its place of origin in Asia to the mission field of Europe. After almost two millennia, Keener reminds us just how relevant this call remains for the growing and vibrant churches of Asia today.

Robert P. Menzies, PhD
Kunming, China

"This is Craig Keener at his best—thoroughly expositional and passionately missional."

Dave Johnson, DMiss
Managing Editor
Asian Journal of Pentecostal Studies

Introduction

It was a special privilege for me to be the speaker for the annual William Menzies lectureship at the Asia Pacific Theological Seminary in Baguio, Philippines, on January 27-30, 2009, on the theme "For All Peoples: A Biblical Theology of Mission." I developed this material from earlier lectures on this theme at two previous institutions: a 2008 Spring Lectureship at the Assemblies of God Theological Seminary in Springfield, Missouri, USA (Jan. 15-17, 2008), and the 2002 Ritter Lecturer for Evangelical Theological Seminary, Myerstown, Pennsylvania, USA.

Although I was working on my Acts commentary at the time I spoke at APTS, it had not yet begun to be published; my John and Matthew commentaries, however, had already been published, with Hendrickson (now with Baker Academic) and Eerdmans, respectively. The articles thus reflect the state of my academic work as it was in 2009—the ideas that went into the Acts commentary are here, but I do not cite it because I wrote the articles first.

Asian Journal of Pentecostal Studies graciously published the lectures as the following articles:

- "Matthew's Missiology: Making Disciples of the Nations (Matt 28:19-20)." *Asian Journal of Pentecostal Studies* 12 (1, Jan. 2009): 3-20.
- "Sent like Jesus: Johannine Missiology (Jn 20:21-22)." *Asian Journal of Pentecostal Studies* 12 (1, Jan. 2009): 21-45.
- "Power of Pentecost: Luke's Missiology in Acts 1—2." *Asian Journal of Pentecostal Studies* 12 (1, Jan. 2009): 47-73.

- "One New Temple in Christ (Eph 2:11-22; Acts 21:27-29; Mk 11:17; Jn 4:20-24)." *Asian Journal of Pentecostal Studies* 12 (1, Jan. 2009): 75-92.

I had earlier published a different article in *AJPS*:
- "Between Asia and Europe: Postcolonial Mission in Acts 16:8-10." AJPS 11 (1-2, 2008): 3-14.

This article offers an example of a specific mission passage in Acts with special relevance to mission in Asia. I hope that I have not overenthusiastically read too much into the passage, but it offers, in any case, a preliminary exploration of a relevant mission question in the New Testament. It thus can provide, in a sense, a fitting climax for the other essays in this volume by illustrating an approach to a particular passage.

I am grateful to the friends at APTS who contributed to the initial journal publication of these studies (Paul Lewis and others), and am grateful to Dave Johnson, who suggested to me the incorporation of these studies into a book on the theme of missiology in the New Testament. Dave and I attended the Assemblies of God Theological Seminary together in Missouri back in the twentieth century, and we discussed the idea for this book when we reunited at the Society for Pentecostal Studies meeting in Cleveland, Tennessee, in March of 2018.

Obviously one could elaborate on this theme in the New Testament at greater length, but my hope is that as a short book (admittedly not typically a trademark of Craig Keener) this one can provide a contribution, on a basic level, to discussion of biblical theology of mission, possibly as a supplemental text in Pentecostal, charismatic or other Spirit-valuing schools.

Chapter 1

Matthew's Missiology: Making Disciples of the Nations (Matt 28:19-20)

M atthew's Gospel closes with what Christians have often called the Great Commission. This commission is no afterthought to his Gospel; rather, it summarizes much of the heart of his message. The earliest audiences of Matthew did not hear snippets extracted from pages in a modern book; they heard the entire Gospel read from a scroll. By the time they got to chapter 28, they would have recognized it as bringing a fitting conclusion to many of the themes appearing throughout that Gospel. As we examine elements of this closing paragraph, we must read it in light of the whole of Matthew that it is intended to climax.[1]

Jesus's last words recorded in this Gospel include one imperative surrounded by three subordinate participial clauses—which is probably to say, one command that's carried out in three ways.[2] The one command is to "make disciples of the nations;" and it is to be implemented by "going," by "baptizing," and by "teaching." In modern church language, we might summarize these global discipleship tasks as cross-cultural ministry, evangelism, and Christian education. Because the Great Commission climaxes Matthew's Gospel, we should read each of these tasks in light of how they are addressed earlier.

---

[1] Much more briefly, I suggested some of these points in Craig S. Keener, *A Commentary on the Gospel of Matthew* (Grand Rapids: Eerdmans, 1999), 715-21 passim; idem, Matthew (IVPNTC; Downers Grove: InterVarsity, 1997), 400-2.

[2] The first participle ("going") may be part of the command ("make disciples"; Cleon Rogers, "The Great Commission," *Bibliotheca Sacra* 130 [1973]: 258-67), but Matthew does often coordinate this participle with the main verb (cf. 2:8; 11:4; 17:27; 28:7; Craig L. Blomberg, *Matthew* [NAC 22; Nashville: Broadman, 1992], 431). Even as an attendant circumstance participle, it remains an essential part of the commission (Daniel B. Wallace, *Greek Grammar Beyond the Basics* [Grand Rapids: Zondervan, 1996], 645).

Going to the Nations

Before commissioning his followers to disciple the nations, Jesus says, "going" (often translated, "as you go"). Because this word evokes Jesus's earlier command to "go" in preaching the kingdom (10:5-7), we can be confident that its use is no accident here. In the earlier passage, however, Jesus's disciples are to go only to Israel's lost sheep and not to Gentile or Samaritan cities (10:5-6),[3] whereas here, the object of going has changed. Jesus's followers are to make disciples of "the nations," so going demands crossing cultural barriers to reach the Gentiles.

Is cross-cultural ministry to Gentiles an idea that Matthew suddenly springs on his predominantly Jewish audience only at the end of his Gospel? Or is it an idea for which he has prepared them throughout? We get a clue by looking first at Matthew's opening genealogy.

Ancient Jewish genealogies typically named only male ancestors, but Matthew includes four women. Of the women he could have included, we might have expected him to mention the most famous— the four matriarchs of Israel (or at least the three who were part of Jesus's royal lineage).[4]   Instead, Matthew includes four women who

---

3"Ways of Gentiles" probably meant roads leading to Gentile cities in or around Palestine (cf. T. W. Manson, *The Sayings of Jesus* [Grand Rapids: Eerdmans, 1979; London: SCM, 1957], 179; Joachim Jeremias, *Jesus's Promise to the Nations* [trans. S. H. Hooke; SBT 24; London: SCM, 1958], 19 n. 3). Samaria and Gentile territories surrounded Galilee; Jesus's instructions thus restricted their immediate mission to Galilee (see Robert H. Gundry, Matthew: *A Commentary on his Literary and Theological Art* [Grand Rapids: Eerdmans, 1982], 185).
4For the fame of the matriarchs, see e.g., *Jub.* 36:23-24; 1Qap Genar 20.2-10; '*Ab. R. Nat.* 26, §54B.

have some sort of association with Gentiles.[5]   Tamar was a Canaanite (Gen 38); ancient Jewish sources acknowledge her as a Gentile.[6] Rahab was from Jericho; in fact, through a series of comparisons, Joshua's narrative contrasts this Gentile (who brought her family into Israel) with the Judahite Achan, whose sin destroyed his family (Josh 2:6-7).[7] Ruth was from Moab; although Moabites officially were not permitted to enter Israel (Deut 23:3), God welcomed her because she followed him (Ruth 1:16). Bathsheba was probably from Judah herself but is named by her deceased husband, Uriah the Hittite, to reinforce her Gentile association. Thus, three ancestors of King David and the mother of King Solomon had some sort of association with Gentiles!

The normal purpose of Jewish genealogies was to emphasize the purity of one's Israelite (or sometimes Levitical) ancestry.[8] By contrast, Matthew specifically highlights the mixed character of Jesus's royal lineage. Why? This genealogy is important. The opening phrase, "book of the generation" (1:1), which appears in Genesis with lists of descendants, Matthew uses to list the ancestors of Jesus. Whereas people normally depend on their ancestors for their existence, Matthew understands that Jesus's ancestors depend on him for their purpose in history.[9]   Yet some of these ancestors were Gentiles. From the very beginning of his Gospel, Matthew shows that Gentiles were

---

[5]With e.g., Eduard Schweizer, *The Good News According to Matthew* (trans. David E. Green; Atlanta: John Knox, 1975), 25; Bo Reicke, *The New Testament Era: The World of the Bible from 500 B.C. to A.D. 100* (trans. David E. Green; Philadelphia: Fortress, 1974), 118; F. F. Bruce, *The Message of the New Testament* (Grand Rapids: Eerdmans, 1981), 65; Gundry, *Matthew*, 15; David Garland, *Reading Matthew: A Literary and Theological Commentary on the First Gospel* (New York: Crossroad, 1993), 18. For early Jewish emphasis on their Gentile character, see e.g., Yair Zakowitch, "Rahab also Mutter des Boas in der Jesus-Genealogie (Matth. I 5)," *Novum Testamentum* 17 (1975): 1-5; Jeremias, *Promise*, 13-14; Marshall D. Johnson, *The Purpose of the Biblical Genealogies: with Special reference to the Setting of the Genealogies of Jesus* (2d ed.; SNTSMS 8; Cambridge: Cambridge University, 1988), 167-70. Some commentators instead associate these women with sexual scandal, but the pattern does not fit Tamar, and miraculous matriarchal births would have better prepared for the virgin birth (1:18-25) than scandalous ones did.

[6]See e.g., *L.A.B.* 9:5; *T. Jud.* 10:6.

[7]E.g., Rahab hides spies on her roof; Achan hides loot beneath his tent; Rahab saves her family by betraying her people, whereas Achan destroys his family by betraying his people; and so forth (see J. Scott Duvall and J. Daniel Hays, *Grasping God's Word* [Grand Rapids: Zondervan, 2001], 297-98).

[8]E.g., Josephus *Apion* 1.30; cf. b. Pes. 62b; p. Ter. 7:1; Johnson 1988: 88-95.

[9]Cf. Gundry, *Matthew*, 10, 13; Daniel Patte, *The Gospel According to Matthew: A Structural Commentary on Matthew's Faith* (Philadelphia: Fortress, 1987), 18.

no afterthought in God's plan, but rather he purposed to bless all the families of the earth in Abraham's seed!

In the very next chapter, those who come to worship the new king of the Jews are the Magi (2:1), Persian astrologers who were supposed to honor especially the Persian king.[10] Their role might have shocked Matthew's audience, who would expect Parthians to be polytheistic[11] and would have recognized the evils of pagan astrology.[12] What underlines the role of the Magi here even more firmly is the contrast with other main characters in the context.[13] Whereas these likely 'pagans' have come to worship the true king (2:2), the current king over Judea—the Idumean Herod—acts like a pagan. Matthew's audience, being a few generations removed from Herod and likely outside Jewish Palestine, might not have known of the many temples Herod built for pagan deities[14] or his reputation for 'eliminating' members of his own

---

[10]Historically, officials did bring congratulations to other rulers (e.g., Josephus *War* 2.309; 4.498-501; Acts 25:13; Ludwig Friedländer, *Roman Life and Manners Under the Early Empire* (4 vols.; trans. from the 7th rev. ed., Leonard A. Magnus, J. H. Freese, and A. B. Gough; New York: Barnes & Noble, 1907-1965), 1:211; Robert F. O'Toole, *Acts 26: The Christological Climax of Paul's Defense [Ac 22:1—26:36]* [AnBib 78; Rome: Biblical Institute, 1978], 16-17); the Magi's visit to Jerusalem probably assumed that the new king was born in the palace (though Bethlehem is only about six miles away; *Student Map Manual: Historical Geography of the Bible Lands* [ed. J. Monson; Grand Rapids: Zondervan; Jerusalem: Pictorial Archive, 1979], 1-1).

[11]See e.g., Josephus *Ant.* 18.348. Some may have been Zoroastrian, but evidence may be lacking that Zoroastrian religion was already as widespread as some scholars suppose (see Edwin M. Yamauchi, *Persia and the Bible*, foreword Donald J. Wiseman [Grand Rapids: Baker, 1996], 395-466; idem, "Did Persian Zoroastrianism Influence Judaism?" 282-97 in *Israel: Ancient Kingdom or Late Invention?*, ed. Daniel I. Block, Bryan H. Cribb and Gregory S. Smith [Nashville: Broadman & Holman Academic, 2008], 291-92).

[12]E.g., *1 En.* 6:7, MSS; 8:3; *Jub.* 8:3; 12:17; 13:16-18; Philo *Praem.* 58; Syr. Men. Sent. 292-93; *Sib. Or.* 3:221-22, 227-29; *Sipra Qed.* pq.6.203.2.1; *Sipre Deut.* 171.4.1; still, astrology exerted a wide influence even in early Judaism (e.g., *Mek. Pisha* 2.44-46). Magi appear negatively in Dan 2:2, 10 LXX; more widely in Theodotian and Aquila; also Josephus *Ant.* 10.195-203.

[13]Ancient audiences were accustomed to comparing characters (on this practice, see e.g., Theon *Progymn.* 2.86-88; Hermog. *Progymn.* 8. On Syncrisis 18-20; Peter Marshall, *Enmity in Corinth: Social Conventions in Paul's Relations with the Corinthians* [WUNT 2, Reihe, 23; Tübingen: J. C. B. Mohr (Paul Siebeck), 1987], 348-53; R. Dean Anderson, Jr., *Glossary of Greek Rhetorical Terms Connected to Methods of Argumentation, Figures and Tropes from Anaximenes to Quintilian* [Leuven: Peeters, 2000], 110-11; Craig S. Keener, *The Gospel of John: A Commentary* (2 vols.; Peabody, MA: Hendrickson, 2003), 916-17, 1183-84).

[14]E.g., Josephus *Ant.* 14.76; 15.298; 16.147; 19.329, 359; *War* 2.266. His building projects and "benefactions" were not, however, limited to Palestine (e.g., *War* 1.422-28).

family[15] or even his murdering of Bethlehem's baby boys (2:16). But ideally they would know Scripture well enough to catch the biblical analogy. By killing these male children, Herod acted like Pharaoh of old (Ex 1:15-22),[16] whereas the Persian wise men honor Israel's true king!

Meanwhile, Herod's own 'wise men' (the chief priests and scribes) knew precisely where the Messiah would be born (2:5-6), yet made no effort to accompany the Magi.[17] Those who knew God's word the best neglected its message—a sin that only Bible readers and teachers can commit. A generation later, their successors became Jesus's most lethal opposition (16:21; 20:18; 27:41). They too stand in contrast to the Magi, who came from afar to worship Israel's rightful king, just as do all Gentiles who become Jesus's followers.

Gentiles continue to surface in Matthew's Gospel. For instance, in chapter 3, John the Baptist reminds the Jewish people that they cannot depend on their ancestry for salvation. Many believed that Abraham's descendants as a whole would be saved;[18] but John tells them God can raise up children for Abraham from stones (3:9)![19] In chapter 4, Jesus relocates to Capernaum, fulfilling a prophecy of Isaiah about "Galilee of the Gentiles" (4:15). In chapter 8, he delivers demoniacs from a largely Gentile region that raises pigs (8:28-34)[20] and heals the servant of a Roman centurion, calling the centurion's faith greater than that of his fellow Israelites (8:10). There Jesus warns that many of Abraham's genetic descendants would perish (8:12), while Gentiles would come from the east (like the Magi) and west (like the Romans) to partake of

---

[15]E.g., *Ant.* 16.394; 17.187, 191; *War* 1.443-44, 550-51, 664-65. For other atrocities or attempted atrocities, see e.g., *Ant.* 17.174-79; *War* 1.437, 659-60. The Herod of Matt 2 acts "in character" with what we know of him historically.

[16]Cf. another pagan king in 1 Macc 1:60-61; 2 Macc 6:10; 8:4.

[17]Historically, the Sanhedrin of Herod's day were his political lackeys, installed after he executed their predecessors (*Ant.* 14.175; 15.2, 5-6).

[18]See especially *m. Sanh.* 10:1.

[19]See more detailed discussion on the background in Keener, *Matthew* (1999), 124-25, and idem, "Human Stones in a Greek Setting: Luke 3.8; Matthew 3.9; Luke 19.40," *Journal of Greco-Roman Christianity and Judaism* 6 (2009): 28-36; for John's preceding denunciation of the religious establishment as the offspring of vipers, see idem, "'Brood of Vipers' (Mt. 3.7; 12.34; 23.33)," *Journal for the Study of the New Testament* 28, no. 1 (Sept. 2005): 3-11.

[20]On Gadara's predominantly Gentile character, cf. e.g., Josephus *Ant.* 17.320; *War* 2.478.

the kingdom banquet with the patriarchs (8:11).[21] Later, Jesus also illustrates north and south, saying that Sheba and Nineveh, which repented, will fare better at the judgment than his generation of Israel, which has not repented (12:41-42).[22] Even wicked Sodom will have a lighter judgment, for they would have repented had they seen the miracles that this generation was seeing (10:15; 11:23-24).[23]

Likewise, Jesus heeds the plea of a Canaanite woman (15:21-28). In Mark, she is a Syro-Phoenician Greek (i.e., a resident of Syrophoenicia belonging to an urbanite ruling class that exploited workers of the countryside), who now comes as a supplicant.[24] Matthew 'overlooks' her credentials but rather identifies her via the fact that she resides in a region populated by descendants of the ancient Canaanites.[25] Matthew's Gospel had opened with the mention of two Canaanite women of faith; this Canaanite also becomes a model of faith, like the Gentile centurion.

It is probably no coincidence that to his disciples Jesus puts the question as to his identity not in Jerusalem or Jewish Galilee but in Caesarea Philippi (16:13), which was a pagan city, originally named

---

[21]The centurion was probably geographically from the eastern empire, perhaps Syria (cf. Josephus *War* 2.267-68; G. H. Stevenson, "The Army and Navy," 218-38 in *The Augustan Empire: 44 B.C.–A.D. 70*, vol. 10 in *The Cambridge Ancient History* [12 vols.; ed. S. A. Cook, F. E. Adcock and M. P. Charlesworth; Cambridge: University Press, 1966], 226-27; John Brian Campbell, "Legion," 839-42 in *OCD*, 839), but he officially represents Rome.

[22]The thought would be intelligible in an early Jewish setting. Some later rabbis suggested that Gentile converts would testify against the nations in the judgment (*Lev. Rab.* 2:9; *Pesiq. Rab.* 35:3), and some found in Nineveh's quick repentance a threat to Israel (*Mek. Pisha* 1.81-82).

[23]The prophets used Sodom to epitomize immorality (Is 13:19; Jer 50:40; Zeph 2:9) and applied the image to Israel (Deut 32:32; Isa 1:10; 3:9; Jer 23:14; Lam 4:6; Ezek 16:46-49). It continued to epitomize immorality in early Judaism (e.g., Sir 16:8; *Jub.* 36:10; 3 Macc 2:5; *t. Sanh.* 13:8; *Shab.* 7:23; *Sipra Behuq.* par. 2.264.1.3; *Sipre Deut.* 43.3.5).

[24]See discussion in Gerd Theissen, *The Gospels in Context: Social and Political History in the Synoptic Tradition* (trans. Linda M. Maloney; Minneapolis: Fortress, 1991), 70-72.

[25]Some find some continuity with Canaanite culture in this period (R. A. Oden, Jr., "The Persistence of Cananite Religion," *Biblical Archaeologist* 39 (1976): 31-36; David Flusser, "Paganism in Palestine," 2:1065-1100 in *The Jewish People in the First Century: Historial Geography, Political History, Social, Cultural and Religious Life and Institutions* [2 vols.; ed. S. Safrai and M. Stern with D. Flusser and W. C. van Unnik; vol. 1: Assen: Van Gorcum & Comp., B.V., 1974; Vol. 2: Philadelphia: Fortress, 1976], 1070-74).

Paneas for its famous grotto of the god Pan.[26] By choosing such a setting, Jesus prefigured the future mission to proclaim his message outside the Holy Lands. It is also undoubtedly no coincidence that the first people to acknowledge Jesus as God's Son after the crucifixion are the Gentile execution squad (27:54).[27]

Lest anyone miss the point of this recurrent theme of Gentiles, Matthew reports Jesus's one prerequisite regarding the end of time. In contrast to the expected end-time signs of his contemporaries (e.g., wars, famines)[28] of which he says "the end is not yet" (24:6-8), Jesus announces that the good news about the kingdom will be proclaimed among all peoples and "then the end will come" (24:14). The closing parable of this discourse reinforces that idea. In 25:31-46, the nations are judged by how they received the messengers of the kingdom, the "least of these my siblings" (25:40, 45). Everywhere else in Matthew, these spiritual siblings represent his disciples (12:49-50; 19:29; 23:8; 28:10); moreover, it is those who receive and give drink to Jesus's agents who are doing the same for him (10:40-42; cf. 10:11).[29] The texts involving proclamation to the nations before "the end" explains why 28:20 emphasizes that Jesus will be with us "until the end of the age." That means he will be with us in the task of discipling the nations (28:19).

---

[26]See Pliny *N.H.* 5.15.71; Josephus *War* 1.404; further Josephus, *The Jewish War* (ed. Gaalya Cornfeld with Benjamin Mazar and Paul L. Maier; Grand Rapids: Zondervan, 1982), 458; Vassilios Tzaferis, "Cults and Deities Worshipped at Caesarea Philippi-Banias," 190-201 in *Priests, Prophets and Scribes: Essays on the Formation and Heritage of Second Temple Judaism in Honour of Joseph Blenkinsopp* (ed. Eugene Ulrich et al., 1992); Vassilios Tzaferis and R. Avner, "Hpyrwt b'ny's," *Qadmoniot* 23, nos. 3-4 (1990). 110-14.

[27]Mark notes only the centurion (Mk 15:39); Matthew broadens this to his colleagues. The detachment for execution may have been as few as four (cf. Acts 12:4; Kirsopp Lake and Henry J. Cadbury, *English Translation and Commentary* [vol. 4 in *The Beginnings of Christianity*; Grand Rapids: Baker, 1979], 134; Philostratus *Vit. Apoll.* 7.31).

[28]Cf. e.g., *Jub.* 23:11-25 (esp. 23:13; 36:1); 1QM 15.1; *Sib. Or.* 3.213-15; *4 Ezra* 8:63-9:8; 13:30; *2 Bar.* 26:1-27:13; 69:3-5; *T. Mos.* 7–8; *m. Sot.* 9:15.

[29]Historically most interpreters applied the passage specifically to believers (whether as the believing poor or, as more often today, to missionaries; for the history of interpretation, see Sherman W. Gray, *The Least of My Brothers: Matthew 25.31-46: A History of Interpretation* [SBLDS 114; Atlanta: Scholars, 1989]).

Many scholars think that Matthew wrote his Gospel after AD 70,[30] in the wake of massive Jewish suffering at the hands of the Gentiles. For those who date Matthew before AD 70,[31] it was nevertheless a period in which tensions were building toward that Judean revolt. Regardless of the date, Matthew's Gospel addresses an audience that has suffered at the hands of Gentiles and likely has every reason to hate them. Yet Matthew's message calls them to cross all barriers in order to reach these very Gentile 'enemies'—even Canaanites and Roman officers. If his Gospel could call that initial audience to lay aside their prejudice in such a way, it certainly can summon us to do no less—to overcome ethnic and cultural prejudice in order to love and serve others no matter what the cost. This is a message of ethnic reconciliation in Christ as well as a summons to global mission.

Baptizing in the Name of the Father, Son, and Holy Spirit

Baptism is an act of repentance, a response to a particular message (as in 3:2-6). For Matthew, the message now inviting baptism reveals the involvement of the triune God in God's kingdom, hence demands submission to the Lordship of Jesus Christ.

Baptism in Matthew's Gospel

When Matthew's audience reaches chapter 28, they can think of the one water baptism already mentioned—John's baptism (3:6), which was meant to prepare for Jesus's greater baptism in the Holy Spirit (3:11). What did John's baptism signify?

Although the Jewish people had many kinds of ceremonial washings, a specific baptism used for a turning from an old way of life

---

[30]E.g., F. F. Bruce, *The New Testament Documents: Are They Reliable?* (5th rev. ed.; Grand Rapids: Eerdmans; Leicester: Inter-Varsity, 1981), 40; Robert H. Mounce, *Matthew* (Good News Commentary; San Francisco: Harper & Row, 1985), xv; W. D. Davies and Dale C. Allison, *A Critical and Exegetical Commentary on the Gospel According to Saint Matthew* (ICC; 3 vols.; Edinburgh: T. & T. Clark, 1988-1997), 1:127-38.

[31]E.g., Gundry, *Matthew*, 599-608; John A. T. Robinson, *Can We Trust the New Testament?* (Grand Rapids: Eerdmans, 1977), 76-78.

to a new one was applied to Gentiles converting to Judaism.[32] As already noted, with respect to salvation, John the Baptist treats his Jewish hearers in the same way that they would treat Gentiles—that is, *all* must come to God on the same terms. Baptism was an act of turning to God, and in baptizing Israel for repentance, John (like the prophets of old) was calling them to turn to God. Baptism was a response to John's message, which is what differentiated it from other kinds of ceremonial washings. Thus, in emulating John's model in baptizing, we are evangelizing (i.e., proclaiming the message of the kingdom and repentance).

The Message of Father, Son, and Spirit

When John baptized, he was inviting people to embrace his message of repentance (3:6; cf. Mk 1:4) and of the kingdom. That is, he was not administering an ordinary proselyte baptism but was baptizing people with respect to a distinctive message. Matthew summarizes both John's and Jesus's message—"Repent, for the kingdom of heaven is at hand" (3:2 and 4:17). And when Jesus sends the Twelve, he commands them to announce that "The kingdom of heaven is at hand" (10:7).

Thus, there is a continuity in the central message concerning the kingdom, a continuity that suggests Matthew expects this proclamation to also be his audience's message. For the Israelites, the good news of God's reign signified the restoration of his people (Isa 52:7) and that he would rule unchallenged. Most Palestinian Jews associated the coming of God's reign with the Davidic Messiah and resurrection from the dead. But we know that the Messiah has both come and is yet to come and that the resurrection has already been inaugurated in history. Therefore, we understand that God, who will consummate his kingdom in the future, has already inaugurated his reign through Jesus's first coming. Matthew balances Jesus's seven parables of the future kingdom

---

[32] For this background, see e.g., H. H. Rowley, "Jewish Proselyte Baptism and the Baptism of John," *HUCA* 15 (1940): 313-34; F. F. Bruce, *New Testament History* (Garden City, NY: Doubleday & Company, 1972), 156; I argue the case in some detail in Keener, *John*, 445-47.

(24:32—25:46) with his seven or eight parables of the present one (13:1-52).[33]

Presumably, other aspects that this passage associates with the kingdom message not revoked later in the Gospel are expected to continue. Signs confirmed God's reign not only in Jesus's ministry (4:23-25), but also in the ministry of his disciples (10:8). In fact, in the context of Jesus's commission in chapter 10, he sends them precisely to multiply his ministry of proclaiming and demonstrating the kingdom (9:35-10:1).[34] Since that objective certainly remains part of the Great Commission, we should expect that God will also provide signs of the kingdom as we work to make disciples of the nations today.[35] While it's unlikely that all of us individually will encounter the same signs to the same degree, we can nevertheless expect God to confirm the true message of the kingdom that we proclaim (cf. Acts 14:3).

However, despite the continuity in our message, ever since Jesus's resurrection, we do have a fuller kingdom message to proclaim. Jesus did imply the "kingdom" when he spoke of authority in 28:18, but now that authority has been delegated to him. Thus, the message of the kingdom is not simply that "heaven" will reign but, more specifically, that the reigning God is Father, Son, and Holy Spirit (28:19). Matthew's Gospel already announced that Jesus had authority on earth to forgive sins (9:6), probably echoing the authority of the Son of Man in Daniel 7:13-14. But now, Jesus has all authority in heaven as well as on earth (28:19); the kingdom of heaven explicitly includes he reign.[36] (Matthew emphasizes Jesus's authority repeatedly before

---

[33]With e.g., Joachim Jeremias, *The Parables of Jesus* (2nd rev. ed.; New York: Charles Scribner's Sons, 1972), 92-93.

[34]See my further comment in Craig Keener, *Gift & Giver: The Holy Spirit for Today* (Grand Rapids: Baker, 2001), 100-1; cf. idem, *The Spirit in the Gospels and Acts: Divine Purity and Power* (Peabody: Hendrickson Publishers, 1997), 110-17.

[35]Besides my *Gift & Giver*, noted above, see more generally e.g., (among many others) John Wimber with Kevin Springer, *Power Evangelism* (San Francisco: Harper & Row, Publishers, 1986); Jack Deere, *Surprised by the Power of the Spirit* (Grand Rapids: Zondervan, 1993); my forthcoming book on *Miracles* (Hendrickson).

[36]Some Jewish texts employ "kingdom of heaven" as periphrasis for "God's kingdom" (*Sipra Qed.* pq. 9.207.2.13; *p. Kid.* 1:2, §24), though these seem particularly characteristic of Matthew. For "heaven" as a familiar Jewish periphrasis for "God," see e.g., Dan 4:26; 3 Macc. 4:21; *1 En.* 6:2; 1QM 12.5; Rom 1:18; Lk 15:18; *m. Ab.* 1:3; *t. B.K.* 7:5; *Sipra Behuq.* pq. 6. 267.2.1; 79.1.1.

climaxing at this point [see 7:29; 8:9; 9:8; 21:27] and his repeated authority over sickness, demons, and nature.)

Moreover, Jesus's promise to be "with them" until the end of the age (28:20) was a divine promise. Judaism acknowledged only God as omnipresent; later, the rabbis called him *makom* ('the place') as a way of emphasizing his omnipresence.[37] But Jesus is with *all* of us in carrying out his commission. This claim climaxes yet another motif in Matthew's Gospel, for the beginning scene announces Jesus as none other than "God with us" (1:23). Later, Jesus tells his disciples that, where two or three are gathered in his name, there he is among them (18:20). This claim recalls a familiar Jewish principle: where two or three gathered to study God's Torah, his Shekinah (presence) was among them.[38] Jesus is thus indicating that he is the very presence of God.

This rank and identity is most explicit in the baptismal message of 28:19 itself. Where John preached a baptism of repentance in light of the coming kingdom, we preach a baptism in the name of the Father, the Son, and the Holy Spirit. Our baptism involves the reign of heaven, which we now understand in terms of the triune God. Jewish people regularly invoked God as Father,[39] and they also recognized the Spirit as divine.[40] So to place the Son between the Father and the Spirit is to claim nothing less than Jesus's deity. When persons are baptized, they should confess Jesus as Lord. When we preach the kingdom now, we can be specific as to who is king in the kingdom of God—Jesus Christ, as well as the Father and the Spirit.

---

[37]E.g., *3 En.* 18:24; *m. Ab.* 2:9, 13; 3:14; *t. Peah* 1:4; 3:8; *Shab.* 7:22, 25; 13:5; *R.H.* 1:18; *Taan.* 2:13; *B.K.* 7:7; *Sanh.* 1:2; 13:1, 6; 14:3, 10; *Sipre Num.* 11.2.3; 11.3.1; 42/1/2; 42.2.3; 76.2.2; 78.1.1; 78.5.1; 80.1.1; 82.3.1; 84.1.1; 84.5.1; 85.3.1; 85.4.1; 85.5.1; *Sipra VDDen.* pq. 2.2.4.2; 4.6.4.1.

[38]*M. Ab.* 3:2, 6; *Mek. Bahodesh* 11.48ff; cf. *m. Ber.* 7:3.

[39]E.g., Sir 23:1, 4; 3 Macc 6:8; *m. Sot.* 9:15; *t. Ber.* 3:14; *B.K.* 7:6; *Hag.* 2:1; *Peah* 4:21; *Sipra Qed.* pq. 9.207.2.13; *Behuq.* pq. 8.269.2.15; *Sipre Deut.* 352.1.2.

[40]In contrast to Christian theology, however, they viewed the Spirit as an aspect of God rather than a distinct divine person (cf. e.g., discussion in Keener, *John*, 961-66; idem, "Spirit, Holy Spirit, Advocate, Breath, Wind," 484-96 in *The Westminster Theological Wordbook of the Bible* [ed. Donald E. Gowan; Louisville, KY: Westminster John Knox, 2003], 484-87, 495-96). It is not impossible that baptism "in the name of the Holy Spirit" might relate somehow (perhaps symbolically) to baptism *in* the Spirit (Matt 3:11), but apart from noting the shared terms I have not yet tried to test this question exegetically.

The immediate context of 28:18-20 offers us another example of proclamation—both positive and negative models. In 28:1-10, Jesus commissions the two women (Mary Magdalene and the other Mary) to carry the message of his resurrection and to bear witness faithfully, which they do, despite the prejudice against a woman's testimony throughout ancient Mediterranean culture.[41] By contrast, in 28:11-15, those who guarded the now-empty tomb, because of fear and greed, bear a false witness.[42] These two models immediately precede the commissioning of the Eleven to make disciples of the nations, a legacy the disciples imparted to those whom they discipled. Thus, the women at the tomb offer the positive model for the church's message, whereas the guards offer the antithesis of that model.[43]

Teaching Them to Obey All that Jesus Commanded

From Matthew's perspective, discipleship is not limited to evangelism; it also includes training those who will be our partners in evangelism. It seems the churches of Asia already understand this, whereas many in North America are weak on both evangelism and training. At least in the United States, the Church has lost much of its emphasis on teaching Scripture, many things instead being driven by marketing. While marketing can be a useful tool, it's not a criterion of truth or morality. Some messages are more popular than others because they're more marketable.

Too many churches across the theological spectrum have succumbed to the culture's values, (e.g., its sexual mores, materialism) or fight for their tradition or focus on charismatic speakers' experiences, etc. And many churches in the West today neglect the very Scriptures that we claim as our arbiters of truth and as living

---

[41]See e.g., Josephus *Ant.* 4.219; *m. Yeb.* 15:1, 8-10; 16:7; *Ket.* 1:6-9; *t. Yeb.* 14:10; *Sipra VDDeho.* pq. 7.45.1.1; Hesiod *W.D.* 375; Livy 6.34.6-7; Babrius 16.10; Phaedrus 4.15; Avianus *Fables* 15-16; Justinian *Inst.* 2.10.6 (though contrast the earlier Gaius *Inst.* 2.105); Plutarch *Publicola* 8.4; cf. Lk 24:11; Craig Keener, *Paul, Women & Wives: Marriage and Women's Ministry in the Letters of Paul* (Peabody, MA: Hendrickson Publishers, 1992), 162-63.

[42]Their fear and greed evoke the failures of Peter (who denied Jesus from fear, 26:70-75) and Judas (who betrayed Jesus from greed, 26:15-16; on the narrative contrasts with Judas in that context, see Keener, *Matthew* [1999], 617, 620).

[43]Keener, *Matthew* (1999), 699, 715.

expressions of God's voice. Syncretism with the world's 'spiritual values,' such as the worship of mammon alongside God, has weakened much of the Church in my nation.

What the Church calls 'missions' is not just about evangelism, but also about training disciples who can partner in the task of evangelism. It must involve multiplying the work by trusting the Holy Spirit and Christ's teaching to multiply equally committed laborers for the harvest.[44]

When Jesus speaks of "teaching them to obey everything I commanded you" (28:20), Matthew's audience will think of the teachings already shared earlier in the Gospel. Many of those teachings are arranged in five major discourse sections,[45] each ending in a clause like, "when Jesus had finished these sayings" (7:28; 11:1; 13:53; 19:1; 26:1).[46] These discourses address the ethics of the kingdom (chapters 5-7), the proclamation of the kingdom (chapter 10), the presence of the kingdom (chapter 13), relationships in the kingdom (chapter 18), and the future of the kingdom from the standpoint of Jesus's first disciples (chapters 23-25). That last section includes the "woes" against the religious establishment as well as the destruction of the temple and judgment of the generation that rejected Jesus. Yet it also looks ahead to judgment on the generation of his second coming, when some of his servants are oblivious to his demands, as was the religious establishment at his first coming (24:45-51; 25:14-30).

Although Matthew's audience might well think of all of Jesus's teachings in this Gospel, I will focus specifically on the ones that concern the "cost of discipleship."[47] Those who are to make disciples of the nations must first understand what discipleship involves. In the

---

[44]See e.g., the biblical strategy in Melvin L. Hodges, *The Indigenous Church* (Springfield, MO: Gospel Publishing House, 1976).

[45]Some have followed Papias in comparing the five sections with the Pentateuch (Bruce, *Documents*, 41; idem, *Message*, 62-63; Peter F. Ellis, *Matthew: His Mind and His Message* [Collegeville, MN: The Liturgical, 1974], 10; Samuel Sandmel, *Anti-Semitism in the New Testament?* [Philadelphia: Fortress, 1978], 51), but most who recognize five sections fail to find this correspondence (Davies and Allison, *Matthew*, 1:61; Donald A. Hagner, *Matthew* [2 vols.; WBC 33AB; Dallas: Word, 1993-1995], 1:li).

[46]Such phrases offered a natural way to close a section; see e.g., Ex 34:33; *Jub.* 32:20; 50:13; Dale C. Allison, *The New Moses: A Matthean Typology* (Minneapolis: Fortress, 1993), 192-93 compares Deut 31:1, 24; 32:45.

[47]For the phrase, see Dietrich Bonhoeffer, *The Cost of Discipleship* (rev. ed.; New York: Macmillan; London: SCM, 1963).

kingdom (as opposed to contemporary models of Jesus's day), his followers are not to make disciples for themselves but only for him, the one true Rabbi (23:8).[48] In the calling of disciples, Jesus made clear that discipleship would require the following "costs":

True disciples must value Jesus above job security. The disciples he called left their nets to follow him. While ordinary fishermen were not among the elite, they were probably better off than the majority of people who were peasant farmers.[49] At least some of them, like Peter, were married (8:14), hence had families to support (since wives earned scant wages in that culture).[50] Thus, to forsake their livelihoods for ministry was a serious act of faith.[51]

True disciples must value Jesus above residential security. Seeing Jesus about to cross the lake, a prospective disciple offers to follow him wherever he goes, "even across this lake"[52] (8:18-19). Despite having a home in Capernaum (4:13), Jesus's itinerant ministry, in a sense, left him no place to rest (8:20),[53] except maybe on a boat during a storm (8:24).[54] Elsewhere, Matthew shows that, even as an infant, Jesus was

---

[48]In Jesus's day, probably an honorary greeting meaning, "my master" (23:7-8). Likewise, "father" (23:9), while a greeting applicable to all elders, was particularly applicable to teachers (2 Kgs 2:12; *4 Bar.* 2:4, 6, 8; 5:5; *t. Sanh.* 7:9; *Sipre Deut.* 34.3.1-3, 5; 305.3.4).

[49]With Sean Freyne, *Galilee, Jesus and the Gospels: Literary Approaches and Historical Investigations* (Philadelphia: Fortress, 1988), 241; cf. John Wilkinson, *Jerusalem as Jesus Knew It: Archaeology as Evidence* (London: Thames and Hudson, 1978), 29-30; Martin Hengel, *Property and Riches in the Early Church: Aspects of Social History of Early Christianity* (Philadelphia: Fortress, 1974), 27.

[50]For women's status in some ancient Mediterranean societies, see e.g., discussion in Sarah B. Pomeroy, *Goddesses, Whores, Wives, and Slaves: Women in Classical Antiquity* (New York: Schocken, 1975); Jane F. Gardner, *Women in Roman Law & Society* (Bloomington: Indiana University, 1986); Tal Ilan, *Jewish Women in Greco-Roman Palestine* (Tübingen: J. C. B. Mohr; Peabody: Hendrickson, 1996); Craig Keener, "Marriage," 680-93 in *Dictionary of New Testament Background* (ed. Craig A. Evans and Stanley E. Porter; Downers Grove, IL: InterVarsity, 2000), 687-90; idem, *Paul, Women & Wives*, passim.

[51]Accounts of people forsaking everything to convert to Judaism (*Sipre Num.* 115.5.7) or philosophy (Diogenes Laertius 6.5.87; Diogenes *Ep.* 38) underlined the value of what the converts were acquiring (cf. Matt 13:44-46).

[52]For the contextual connection, see Jack Dean Kingsbury, "On Following Jesus: the 'Eager' Scribe and the 'Reluctant' Disciple (Matthew 8.18-22)," *New Testament Studies* 34 (1988): 45-59, here 56.

[53]His comparison with birds (cf. Ps 11:1; 84:3; 102:6-7; 124:7; Prov 27:8; at Qumran, cf. Otto Betz, *What Do We Know About Jesus?* [Philadelphia: Westminster; London: SCM, 1968], 72) and foxes (Lam 5:18; Ezek 13:4) is apt, since they lacked much residential security; he lacked more.

[54]It might be noteworthy that Matthew omits the makeshift cushion in Mk 4:38.

a refugee (2:13-15). Thus, those who follow him will have no certain home in this world.

True disciples must value Jesus above financial security. Jesus admonished a rich young man who wanted eternal life to give everything he had to the poor (19:21). Radical teachers in antiquity sometimes tested their would-be disciples to see if they were willing to count the cost.[55] But the principle in Jesus's demand extends beyond this particular rich man. He summons all his disciples to lay up treasures in heaven rather than on earth (6:19-21)[56] and to concern themselves with the affairs of the kingdom rather than with the source of their food or drink (6:24-34).

True disciples must value Jesus above social obligations. Wishing to defer discipleship, one prospective disciple tells Jesus he wants to first bury his father. Jesus's seemingly curt response is for this man to follow him now and leave the burying to others (8:21-22). In those days, on learning that his father had died, a son would have gone home immediately and would not have even been talking with Jesus. Likely the son is asking for either of two things as a delaying tactic. One possibility was for as much as a year's delay; after the initial burial and seven days of mourning,[57] he would need to remain available for the secondary burial a year later.[58] The other possibility was for an indefinite delay; in a related Middle Eastern idiom, one can speak of fulfilling a final filial obligation with reference to the father's future death (meaning here that the father might not even have died yet).[59]

Whichever of the two was more likely, neither would significantly reduce the social scandal of Jesus's demand, for many Jewish sages

---

[55]E.g., Diogenes Laertius 6.2.36, 75-76; 6.5.87; 7.1.22; cf. Aulus Gellius 19.1.7-10. Such teachers intended these challenges as tests, not absolute rejection; they normally accepted as disciples those who agreed to their demands (Diogenes Laertius 6.2.21; Diogenes *Ep.* 38; cf. *Sipre Num.* 115.5.7).

[56]Jesus adapted widely used language and imagery here (e.g., Sir 29:10-11; *4 Ezra* 7:77; *2 Bar.* 14:12; 24:1; 44:14; *t. Peah* 4:18).

[57]Cf. Sir 22:12; Jdt 16:24; S. Safrai, "Home and Family," 728-92 in *Jewish People in the First Century*, 782.

[58]See Byron R. McCane, "'Let the Dead Bury Their Own Dead': Secondary Burial and Matt 8:21-22," *Harvard Theological Review* 83 (1990): 31-43.

[59]Kenneth Ewing Bailey, *Through Peasant Eyes: More Lucan Parables, Their Culture and Style* (Grand Rapids: Eerdmans, 1980), 26.

considered honoring parents a son's greatest responsibility,[60] and burying them was perhaps the greatest expression of that responsibility.[61] Only God himself could take precedence over parents in such a matter![62] A son who failed to fulfill this task would be ostracized in his home village for the rest of his life. Notwithstanding, the call to follow Jesus, who is "God with us" (1:23), takes priority over social obligations and honor.

Yet all the costs of discipleship pale in comparison to the ultimate demand Jesus places on prospective followers. For those who want to be his disciples must take up their cross and follow him—to the cross (16:24). In Jesus's day, when people spoke of "going to the cross," they normally meant being led to execution, often through a hostile mob.[63] Jesus demands nothing less than his followers' lives.

While there may be an element of hyperbole in some of Jesus's teachings,[64] the point of hyperbole is not so that hearers will dismiss it lightly as simply hyperbole, as it is sometimes portrayed today. The point of hyperbole is to challenge the hearers. Nevertheless, while Jesus's standard is an absolute one, it is implemented with grace, as Matthew's narratives reveal. Jesus warned that a true disciple must follow him to the cross. However, even his first disciples abandoned him and fled (26:56), their failure leaving the Romans to 'draft' a bystander (Simon of Cyrene) to carry the cross that Jesus's disciples failed to carry for him (27:32).[65] Yet he never repudiated his disciples. Instead, he patiently molded them into what he had called them to be.

---

[60]*Let. Arist.* 228; Josephus *Apion* 2.206; Ps.-Phoc. 8; George Foot Moore, *Judaism in the First Centuries of the Christian Era* (2 vols.; New York: Schocken, 1971), 2:132.

[61]E.g., Tob 4:3-4; 6:14; 1 Macc 2:70; 4 Macc 16:11. Failure to bury a father was offensive throughout Mediterranean antiquity (e.g., Demosth. *Against Aristogeiton* 54).

[62]Deut 13:6; 4 Macc 2:10-12; Josephus *Apion* 2.206; Ps.-Phoc. 8; *b. Meg.* 3b. Some teachers claimed priority over parents (e.g., *m. B.M.* 2:11; cf. Diodorus Siculus 10.3.4), but not to the extent of damaging funeral arrangements!

[63]Jeremias, *Parables*, 218-19; idem, *New Testament Theology* (New York: Charles Scribner's Sons, 1971), 242.

[64]A common ancient pedagogic device (e.g., *Rhet. Her.* 4.33.44; Cicero *Orator* 40.139; Philostratus *V.A.* 8.7; *Hrk.* 48.11; R. Dean Anderson, Jr., *Glossary of Greek Rhetorical Terms*, 122-24. Galen O. Rowe, "Style," 121-57 in *Handbook of Classical Rhetoric in the Hellenistic Period 330 B.C.—A.D. 400* [ed. Stanley E. Porter; Leiden: Brill, 1997], 128).

[65]Keener, *Matthew* (1999), 676. On Simon of Cyrene, see e.g., Raymond E. Brown, *The Death of the Messiah: From Gethsemane to Grave. A Commentary on the Passion Narratives in the Four Gospels* (2 vols.; New York: Doubleday, 1994), 913.

Likewise, fully aware of what we are made of, Jesus can nonetheless make us into what he has called us to be.

Conclusion

Matthew 28:19-20 pulls together some major themes that run through the rest of the Gospel. Its one command—making disciples of the nations—involves three elements found in subordinate participial clauses. These are going, baptizing, and teaching. Each of the themes implied in these phrases appears throughout the Gospel. Matthew repeatedly emphasizes the role of Gentiles (1:3-6; 2:1-2; 8:10-12; 15:21-28; 24:14; 27:54; cf. 3:9; 4:15; 8:28; 10:15; 11:23-24; 12:41-42; 16:13; 25:32), hence cross-cultural concern. John's baptism involved the message of the kingdom (3:2; cf. 4:17; 10:7); but the Gospel climaxes by declaring a baptism the message of which reveals the fullness of God that Christian tradition calls the Trinity.[66] Jesus, who has all authority, is king in God's kingdom (28:18), is linked with the Father and Spirit (28:19), and is with his people (28:20) as "God with us" (1:23; 18:20). The two women and the guards provide contrasting models for announcing Jesus's message (28:1-15). Lastly, the Gospel is replete with Jesus's teachings, including not only five discourse sections, but also other specific teachings on the cost of discipleship relevant to the new mission (e.g., 4:19-20; 8:20, 22; 16:24; 19:21).

This survey offers implications for the Church's missionary task. The Great Commission is not an idea Matthew tacked inelegantly to the end of his Gospel as if he had nowhere else to put it. Rather, it summarizes the heart of this Gospel's message. The question it presents to us as believers today is whether we will devote our lives to what Christ has commanded.

Each of us has different gifts and callings, but we must organize those gifts around this central task. Like a nation devoted to some all-consuming war, we must engage in total mobilization, bringing to bear

---

[66]The term may stem from the late second-century North African theologian Tertullian (see e.g., R. L. Richard, "Trinity, Holy," 14:293-306 in *New Catholic Encyclopedia* [17 vols.; Washington, D.C.: Catholic University of America, 1967], 297), but the idea is already present early in the New Testament (see e.g., Gordon D. Fee, *God's Empowering Presence: The Holy Spirit in the Letters of Paul* [Peabody: Hendrickson, 1994], 839-42).

all of our resources for this mission. Our conflict, though, is a spiritual one, not with flesh and blood, and it invites us to devote all that we are and have to mobilize the Church to fulfill Christ's mission. Never before have the stakes been so high. Some estimate that the world's population was one billion by 1830 and two billion by 1930; it is close to seven billion today. God's power will be commensurate with the task he gives us. Are we ready?

Chapter 2

Sent Like Jesus:
Johannine Missiology
(Jn 20:21-22)

Although scholars sometimes treat John as the most universal of the Gospels (cf. Jn 19:20), it (along with Matthew) is the most distinctively Jewish and the most explicitly rooted in Judean topography and culture.[1] But while it specifically views the hostile world through the lens of Judean authorities, that world is theologically a wider one.

We could thus treat Johannine missiology through the lens of some other texts, such as John 3:16; but we will subsume that text under our larger discussion outlined in John 20:21-22. As with the other lectures/articles in this series, I am using a single passage, here John 20, to provide a structure for addressing the themes of the entire book or body of literature in which they appear.[2] When John's first audience

---

[1]As has been long and widely noted, e.g., Wayne A. Meeks, "'Am I a Jew?'— Johannine Christianity and Judaism," 1:163-186 in *Christianity, Judaism and Other Greco-Roman Cults: Studies for Morton Smith at Sixty* (4 vols.; ed. Jacob Neusner; SJLA 12; Leiden: Brill, 1975), 1:163; D. Moody Smith, "What Have I Learned about the Gospel of John?" 217-35 in *"What Is John?" Readers and Readings of the Fourth Gospel* (ed. Fernando F. Segovia; SBL Symposium Series 3; Atlanta: Scholars Press, 1996), 218-22; James H. Charlesworth, "The Dead Sea Scrolls and the Gospel According to John," 65-97 in *Exploring the Gospel of John: In Honor of D. Moody Smith*; ed. R. Alan Culpepper and C. Clifton Black; Louisville: Westminster John Knox, 1996); J. Louis Martyn, "Source Criticism and Religionsgeschichte in the Fourth Gospel (1970)," 99-121 in *The Interpretation of John* (ed. John Ashton; Issues in Religion and Theology 9; Philadelphia: Fortress; London: S.P.C.K., 1986); John A. T. Robinson, *Can We Trust the New Testament?* (Grand Rapids: Eerdmans, 1977), 82; W. D. Davies, "Reflections on Aspects of the Jewish Background of the Gospel of John," 43-64 in *Exploring the Gospel of John: In Honor of D. Moody Smith*; David Flusser, *Judaism and the Origins of Christianity* (Jerusalem: Magnes, Hebrew University, 1988), 23-24.

[2]I treat this approach of reading each part in light of the whole on a very basic level in Craig Keener, *Biblical Interpretation* (Springfield, MO: Africa Theological Training Service, 2005), 45-66.

finally reached chapter 20, they would be hearing it in the light of all that had gone before.

When the risen Christ appears to the disciples, he commissions them to carry on his work— "As the Father has sent me, in the same way I have sent you" (v. 21). Then he empowers them to do it— "Receive the Holy Spirit" (v. 22). Thus, this passage involves three primary elements relevant to our discussion of Johannine missiology— the model of Jesus, the empowerment of the Spirit, and the mission of Jesus's followers. The Spirit and Jesus's followers together carry on aspects of Jesus's mission. What then was that mission?

"As the Father Has Sent Me" (20:21)

Jesus kept telling his disciples that he was going to go to the Father and then return to them so that they could enter the Father's presence. Although his long-term ascension (20:17) may still remain future in our passage,[3] Jesus has already gone to the Father by dying, preparing a place for them in the Father's presence (14:2-6, 23). Now he has returned and commissions them to carry on his mission. He sends them *kathōs*—i.e., "in the same way" that the Father sent him.[4] If we wish to understand what the text means by his followers being sent, we must first examine the explicit model for their sending in the ministry of Jesus.

"Sending" in John's Gospel

The motif of "agency" (or being sent) is frequent in John's Gospel.[5] A text very much like this one appears in 13:20—"Whoever receives whomever I send receives me; whoever receives me receives him who

---

[3]See discussion (and a survey of alternatives) in Craig S. Keener, *The Gospel of John: A Commentary* (2 vols.; Peabody, MA: Hendrickson, 2003), 1192-95 (also discussing the function of narrative predictions in ancient literature).

[4]Roughly 17.3% of this adverb's NT appearances are in John's Gospel, whereas this Gospel constitutes only 11% of the NT text, so John uses the adverb roughly 36.4% more than average. The Johannine epistles account for 7% of NT uses, though they constitute only about 1.7% of the NT text; thus they use it over 400% more than average (though these letters' sample size is too small to draw firm stylistic conclusions).

[5]See discussion in Keener, *John*, 310-17, here especially 315-17.

sent me."[6] Jesus's followers carry out his mission as he carries out the Father's. The concept may be implicit even in John's terms for sending, insofar as those terms reflect a special Jewish tradition about what it means to send someone. Contrary to some scholarly traditions, John's two Greek terms for "send" are interchangeable, and he employs both for the Father sending the Son and for the Son sending the disciples.

In antiquity, those sent with a commission were authorized representatives (agents) of those who sent them, and how one treated those agents would reflect one's attitude toward the sender.[7] Later, rabbis even came up with specific rules regarding commissioned agents, including the formulation, "A person's agent is as the person himself."[8] The agent carried the full authority of the sender to the extent that the agent accurately represented the sender's commission.[9] Jewish people recognized Moses[10] and the prophets[11] as God's agents who were sent with his message.

Verbs for "sending" appear some sixty times in John's Gospel. They were applicable to John the Baptist (1:6, 33; 3:28), to agents of the authorities (1:19, 22, 24; 5:33; 7:32), to the disciples (4:38; 13:20; 17:18), and to the advocate, the Spirit (14:26; 15:26; 16:7). But most often, they were applicable to Jesus as the agent of the Father (3:17, 34;

---

[6]This same language appears in different words in Matt 10:40 (probably "Q" material; see Lk 10:16); cf. Mk 9:37.

[7]See Diodorus Siculus 4.10.3-4; Josephus *Ant.* 8.220-21; more fully, Keener, *John*, 313-14.

[8]See *m. Ber.* 5:5; *t. Taan.* 3:2; *b. Naz.* 12b. For the Jewish custom as relevant to the NT, see especially Karl Heinrich Rengstorf, *Apostolate and Ministry* (St. Louis: Concordia Publishing House, 1969); on Johannine and rabbinic "sending," H. S. Friend, "Like Father, Like Son. A Discussion of the Concept of Agency in Halakah and John," *Ashland Theological Journal* 21 (1990): 18-28. Despite detractors, most scholars today accept the connection (noted also by W. D. Davies and Dale C. Allison, *A Critical and Exegetical Commentary on the Gospel According to Saint Matthew* [ICC; 3 vols.; Edinburgh: T. & T. Clark, 1988-1997], 2:153); some church fathers also recognized the connection (see J. B. Lightfoot, *St Paul's Epistle to the Galatians* [3d ed.; London: Macmillan & Company, 1869], 93-94; Gregory Dix, *The Apostolic Ministry* [ed. Kenneth E. Kirk; London: Hodder & Stoughton, 1947], 228). It might be better to view rabbinic and Johannine agency as particular cases of a larger ancient Mediterranean conception.

[9]On agents being backed by the sender's authority, see e.g., Dionysius of Halicarnassus 6.88.2; Diodorus Siculus 40.1.1; Josephus *Life* 65, 72-73, 196-98; 2 Macc 1:20.

[10]E.g., Exod 3:10, 13-15; 4:28; 7:16; Deut 34:11; *Sipra Behuq.* pq. 13.277.1.13-14; *'Ab. R. Nat.* 1 A, most MSS.

[11]E.g., 2 Sam 12:1; 2 Kgs 17:13; 2 Chron 24:19; 25:15; 36:15; Jer 7:25; 24:4; 26:5; 28:9; 35:15; 44:4; Bar 1:21; *Mek. Pisha* 1.87; *'Ab. R. Nat.* 37, §95 B.

4:34; 5:23-24, 30, 36-38; 6:29, 38-39, 44, 57; 7:16, 28-29, 33; 8:16, 18, 26, 29, 42; 9:4; 10:36; 11:42; 12:44-45, 49; 13:20; 14:24; 15:21; 16:5; 17:3, 8, 18, 21, 23, 25). In these passages, Jesus consistently defers all honor for his mission to his sender (cf. 7:18). He recognizes that an agent (like a servant) is never greater than the sender (Jn 13:16).[12]   Thus, full submission to the Father's purpose and deferring all honor to him are two ways that Jesus models what it means to be divinely commissioned.

Jesus as God's Revealer

Jesus came to reveal the Father's heart. As he says in 12:45, "Whoever beholds me beholds the one who sent me." John has been sharing this message since the opening of his Gospel, which climaxes in the announcement that Jesus has revealed God to us (1:18). John's prologue is framed with the twin claims that Jesus is deity and that he is in absolute intimacy with the Father (1:1-2, 18).[13] Unlike Jesus, we are not deity, but Jesus's invitation to abide in him is an invitation to intimacy with him as the basis for our mission (15:4-5).

Also in the Gospel's prologue, Jesus so accurately reflects the Father that he is the Father's logos (normally translated "Word"). John draws here on a range of rich Greek and Jewish concepts,[14] but most fundamentally the term for Jewish hearers would evoke God's revelation of himself in Scripture (especially in the law) as God's Word.[15] Yet Jesus is a fuller, deeper revelation than was available in the law. In the climax of his prologue, John compares Jesus with the

---

[12]On the Son's submission as the Father's agent, see e.g., Craig S. Keener, "Is Subordination Within the Trinity Really Heresy? A Study of John 5:18 in Context," *Trinity Journal* 20 NS, no. 1 (Spring 1999): 39-51, here 45-47.

[13]Marie-Emile Boismard, *St. John's Prologue* (trans. Carisbrooke Dominicans; London: Blackfriars Publications, 1957), 76-77.

[14]See the survey of Greek conceptions in Keener, *John*, 341-43; for Philo, ibid., 343-47; and for more traditional Jewish conceptions, ibid., 347-63.

[15]Keener, *John*, 359-63; Eldon Jay Epp, "Wisdom, Torah, Word: The Johannine Prologue and the Purpose of the Fourth Gospel," 128-46 in *Current Issues in Biblical and Patristic Interpretation: Studies in Honor of Merrill C. Tenney Presented by his Former Students* (ed. Gerald F. Hawthorne; Grand Rapids: Eerdmans, 1975); in the Gospel more generally, see Dan Lidy, *Jesus as Torah in John 1–12* (Eugene: Wipf & Stock, 2007).

Torah (hence Jesus's first witnesses with Moses) as the following chart illustrates:[16]

Exodus 32-33	John 1:14-18
The giving of the law	The giving of the Word
God "dwelt" among his people in the wilderness	The Word "tabernacled" among us (1:14)
Moses beheld God's glory	We beheld his glory (1:14)
The glory revealed God's goodness (33:19) and was "abounding in covenant love and truth" (34:6)	His glory was "full of grace and truth" (1:14)
Although grace and truth were present, Moses could not withstand God's full glory (33:20-23)	The law was given through Moses, but the fullness of grace and truth came through Jesus Christ (1:17)
No one can behold God (33:20)	No one has ever seen God—but now the only Son of God, in intimate communion with the Father, has unveiled his character fully (1:18)

The glory that Moses beheld only in part, the disciples discovered fully in Jesus, although in a hidden way. The glory at his first coming did not look outwardly like the glory on Mount Sinai, but in terms of revealing God's character and heart, it went beyond Sinai. What does this glory look like in John's Gospel?

If we trace the terminology of "glory" throughout his Gospel, we see that Jesus's glory and character were revealed in his various kind

---

[16]With many, e.g., Boismard, *Prologue*, 135-45, especially 136-39; Jacob J. Enz, "The Book of Exodus as a Literary Type for the Gospel of John," *Journal of Biblical Literature* 76 (1957): 208-15, here 212; Peder Borgen, *Bread from Heaven: An Exegetical Study of the Concept of Manna in the Gospel of John and the Writings of Philo* (Leiden: E. J. Brill, 1965), 150-51; Anthony Hanson, "John I.14-18 and Exodus XXXIV," *New Testament Studies* 23, no. 1 (Oct. 1976): 90-101; Everett F. Harrison, "A Study of John 1:14," 23-36 in *Unity and Diversity in NT Theology: Essays in Honor of G. E. Ladd* (ed. Robert A. Guelich; Grand Rapids: Eerdmans, 1978), 29; Henry Mowvley, "John 1.14-18 in the Light of Exodus 33.7-34.35," *Expository Times* 95, no. 5 (Feb. 1984): 135-37.

works (e.g., 2:11), but that the ultimate expression of his glory appears in 12:23-24—Jesus will be glorified by laying down his life.[17] The ultimate expression of God's grace and truth, too glorious even for Moses to see, emerged where the world's hatred for God also came to its ultimate expression. As we pounded the nails into the hands of God's own Son, he was crying, "I love you! I love you! I love you!" In the incarnation (and ultimately in the cross), Jesus revealed God's heart to us.

Jesus as Unique, Jesus as Model

There are some ways, of course, in which the Father's sending of the Son is *unique*. Jesus is the *monogenēs* (1:14, 18; 3:16, 18; 1 Jn 4:9), the specially beloved and unique Son. (The traditional English translation, "only-begotten," reads too much etymology into the term).[18] We are not divine; so although the world is to see God among us (13:34-35; 17:21, 23), we are not his revealers in the unique way that Jesus was. While we may lay down our lives for one another (1 Jn 3:16), we do not carry away the sin of the world (John 1:29). John declares that the Father sent the Son not to condemn the world but to save it (3:17). Jesus's agents do not save the world, but instead, like John the Baptist in the prologue (1:7), are sent to bear witness concerning the light (e.g., 15:27).

Still, John shows that the role as Jesus's agents is indispensable, because others would believe through their message (17:20) and, as we shall soon propose, the Holy Spirit would "prosecute" the world through their witness for him (16:7-11). Even the context of our primary text (20:21-22) emphasizes that Jesus's agents are stewards of

---

[17]With e.g., Gary M. Burge, *The Anointed Community: The Holy Spirit in the Johannine Tradition* (Grand Rapids: Eerdmans, 1987), 132-33; David Earl Holwerda, *The Holy Spirit and Eschatology in the Gospel of John: A Critique of Rudolf Bultmann's Present Eschatology* (Kampen: J. H. Kok, 1959), 5-8; F. F. Bruce, *The Message of the New Testament* (Grand Rapids: Eerdmans, 1981), 105; W. Nicol, "The History of Johannine Research during the Past Century," *Neotestamentica* 6 (1972): 8-18, here 16.

[18]See R. L. Roberts, "The Rendering 'Only Begotten' in John 3:16," *Restoration Quarterly* 16 (1973): 2-22, here 4; I. J. Du Plessis, "Christ as the 'Only Begotten,'" *Neotestamentica* 2 (1968): 22-31; G. Pendrick, "Monogenēs," *New Testament Studies* 41, no. 4 (1995): 587-600; Harrison, "John 1:14," 32.

God's forgiveness (20:23), presumably by accurately representing him (cf. 16:7-11).[19]

Nevertheless, provided that we allow for Jesus's unique role and status, John's Gospel also presents him as a model for mission and demonstrates that those he sends come to participate in that mission. In 1:43-45, Jesus called Philip to follow him, and he followed Jesus's example by testifying to Nathanael from his experience understood through Scripture. But it's the encounter with Jesus himself that converts—for example, Philip invites Nathanael to "Come and see" (1:46), and Nathanael believes as a result of meeting Jesus, who knows his life (1:46-51).

Similarly, in 4:26, Jesus reveals his identity to a Samaritan woman, who, in turn, invites her entire town to "Come, see" the one who knew her life (4:29). Afterward, although they initially accept the woman's testimony (4:39),[20] more Samaritans believe more fully once they meet Jesus themselves (4:41-42). As in Nathanael's case, it is experiencing Jesus personally that converts them—all of which confirms that the honor cannot go to the witnesses. We are Jesus's agents; but as Jesus honored the Father, we are to honor the Son. It is as we introduce people to his living presence that they become most fully confronted by his truth, whether that makes them more hostile or more receptive.

"Sent" to "the World" (3:16-17)

In 20:21, Jesus does not specify to whom he is sent, but this object is clear from earlier passages in the Gospel. It repeatedly emphasizes that the Father sent Jesus "to the world" (3:17; 10:36; 17:18; cf. 8:26; 17:21, 23), a theme repeated in 1 John 4:9, 14. The stated purpose of this sending is that the world might be saved (Jn 3:17; 1 Jn 4:14; cf. Jn 6:33, 51; 1 Jn 4:9).[21]

---

[19]Cf. e.g., James I. Cook, "John 20:19-23, An Exegesis," *Reformed Review* 21, no. 4 (Dec. 1967): 2-10, here 7-8.

[20]Despite the typical prejudice against women's testimony in Mediterranean antiquity; see e.g., Josephus *Ant.* 4.219; *m. Yeb.* 15:1, 8-10; 16:7; *Ket.* 1:6-9; *t. Yeb.* 14:10; *Sipra VDDeho.* pq. 7.45.1.1; Hesiod *W.D.* 375; Livy 6.34.6-7; Babrius 16.10; Phaedrus 4.15; Avianus *Fables* 15-16; Justinian *Inst.* 2.10.6.

[21]Although Jesus came not with the purpose of condemning the world (3:17; 12:47), his coming does precipitate judgment (9:39; 16:8, 11).

John 3:16-17 states God's motive in sending Jesus to the world—God loved the world.[22] In contrast to some attempts to distinguish the meanings of the two Greek words (*phileō* and *agapaō*) used for "love," John employs them interchangeably for literary variation, as was common in his day.[23] Both verbs apply to Jesus's love for the Father, the Father's love for Jesus, and virtually every other category of love in the Gospel. What tells us about the character of divine love is not whether John uses *phileō* or *agapaō*, but how he defines this love in the context. "So" (*houtōs*) here does not say that God loved the world so *much*, but rather that this is *how* God loved the world[24]—He gave his Son.

While a good human father loves his sons, we should understand that God the Father loves his Son infinitely, no less than himself. Yet he and the Son together[25] sacrificed this Son so that the world might have life. This means that God loves the world (or those who would become his own out of the world) no less infinitely. As Jesus later says to the disciples, his followers' unity would reveal divine love to the

---

[22]On divine love originating the sending in John's theology, see M. Waldstein, "Die Sendung Jesu und der Jünger im Johannesevangelium," *Internationale Katholische Zeitschrift/Communio* 19, no. 3 (1990): 203-21. For God's love focused especially on the righteous or Israel, see e.g., CD 8.17; *'Ab. R. Nat.* 36, §94B; *Sipra Deut.* 97.2; further discussion in Keener, *John*, 568-69.

[23]With most scholars today: e.g., John Painter, *John: Witness and Theologian* (foreword by C. K. Barrett; London: S. P. C. K., 1975), 62, 92; F. F. Bruce, *The Gospel of John: Introduction, Exposition and Notes* (Grand Rapids: Eerdmans, 1983), 404; Andrew T. Lincoln, *The Gospel According to Saint John* (BNTC; Peabody: Hendrickson, 2005), 517-18; Charles H. Talbert, *Reading John: A Literary and Theological Commentary on the Fourth Gospel and the Johannine Epistles* (New York: Crossroad, 1992), 261; R. H. Lightfoot, *St. John's Gospel: A Commentary* (ed. C. F. Evans; London: Oxford University Press, 1960), 343; Anthony C. Thiselton, "Semantics and New Testament Interpretation," 75-104 in *New Testament Interpretation: Essays on Principles and Methods* (ed. I. Howard Marshall; Grand Rapids: Eerdmans, 1977), 93; R. Alan Culpepper, *The Gospel and Letters of John* (Nashville: Abingdon, 1998), 248; Herman N. Ridderbos, *The Gospel according to John: A Theological Commentary* (trans. John Vriend; Grand Rapids: Eerdmans, 1997), 665-66. For the commonness of literary variation in antiquity, see e.g., Cicero *Orator* 46.156-57; *Fam.* 13.27.1; Aulus Gellius 1.4; R. Dean Anderson, Jr., *Glossary of Greek Rhetorical Terms Connected to Methods of Argumentation, Figures and Tropes from Anaximenes to Quintilian* (Leuven: Peeters, 2000), 53-54, 114.

[24]With Robert H. Gundry and Russell W. Howell, "The Sense and Syntax of John 3:14-17 with Special Reference to the Use of houtōs . . . hōste in John 3:16," *Novum Testamentum* 41, no. 1 (1999): 24-39.

[25]John emphasizes that the Son laid down his life voluntarily (Jn 6:51; 10:11, 15, 17-18; cf. 15:13), inviting his followers to do the same (1 Jn 3:16).

world, so that the world would recognize that God loved the disciples, even as he loved Jesus (17:23).

God's love is no mere abstraction, no empty words. Rather, he demonstrated that love in an act. The act in which God "loved" the world was that he "gave" his Son. The aorist verb tense for both loved and gave might point to this single act, which the context indicates as being the cross (3:14-15).[26] Just as Paul emphasized decades before John's Gospel, God demonstrated his love for us through the death of his Son while we were his enemies (Rom 5:8-10).

The necessary condition God requires for eternal life is stated as "trust." The rest of John's Gospel and possibly the verb tense indicate that this trust requires persevering faith (Jn 8:31; 15:6), in contrast to the inadequate faith earlier in this context (2:23-25). The rest of John's Gospel also defines the object of faith, which ultimately recognizes Jesus as our Lord and God (20:28). Here then we have the motivation, the method, and the message for our mission—i.e., motivated by God's love (cf. 2 Cor 5:14), we lay down our lives to invite people to trust (depend on, entrust themselves to, declare loyalty to) God's Son, the Lord Jesus Christ.

Especially note here the object of God's love—"the world." In John's Gospel, the world often represents humanity hostile toward God (1:10; 3:19; 7:7; 8:23; 12:25, 31; 14:17, 19, 22, 30; 15:18-19; 16:11, 20, 33; 17:14, 25); yet it is out of that hostile world that he saves those who trust in him (13:1; 17:6, 9, 11, 14-16, 25).[27] After this passage, the next mention of "the world" comes in 4:42, where Samaritans recognize

---

[26]Cf. also e.g., Ernest Evans, "The Verb *agapan* in the Fourth Gospel," 64-71 in *Studies in the Fourth Gospel* (ed. F. L. Cross; London: A. R. Mowbray & Company, 1957), 68; Raymond E. Brown, *The Gospel According to John* (2 vols.; Anchor Bible 29 and 29A; Garden City, NY: Doubleday & Company, 1966-1970), 1:133.

[27]Just as only a Samaritan (4:9) and a Gentile (18:35) acknowledge Jesus as a Jew, it is especially the most hostile representatives of "the world" who recognize that "the world" (much of humanity) goes after Jesus (11:48; 12:19). John thus mitigates his portrayal of the "world's" hostility on a personal level: the world may come to know about God, i.e., so some will be saved (14:31; 17:21, 23; 13:35); Jesus's death invites "all people" (12:32); the Judean crowds are divided in their responses to Jesus (7:43; 9:16; 10:19); Jesus invites the world (18:36-37).

Jesus as savior of the world.[28] Jesus crossed multiple barriers,[29] most obviously the ethnic and cultural ones (4:9), to bring eternal life to the Samaritan woman at the well, who, in turn, brought her people to Jesus. While John's 'narrative world' does not venture directly beyond the Samaritans, it does imply the world beyond them. For Jesus has "other sheep who are not of this fold" (10:16; cf. 7:35),[30]—i.e., those who will believe in him through his disciples' message (17:20). John's mention of the "world," then, is as much a summons to reach all peoples as Matthew's or Luke's call to the "nations." Isaiah's light to the nations (42:6; 49:6; cf. 60:2-3) is in John's Gospel the light of the world (8:12; 9:5; 11:9; 12:46).

"Receive the Holy Spirit" (20:22)

In this Gospel, not only are Jesus and his disciples "sent," but so is the Holy Spirit, who comes to represent and carry on Jesus's work. In 14:26, the Spirit is sent in Jesus's name, and in 15:26, he is sent to bear witness to Jesus. Thus, we are able to carry on Jesus's mission only because God himself lives and works in us. No sooner does Jesus give the disciples the commission than he breathes on them and commands them to "Receive the Holy Spirit" (20:22). Just as in 15:26-27 and 16:7, the Spirit is closely connected with the disciples' witness.

---

[28]On the implied ethnic universalism, see e.g., Francis J. Moloney, *Belief in the Word; Reading the Fourth Gospel, John 1-4* (Minneapolis: Fortress, 1993), 14.

[29]See Keener, *John*, 585; idem, "Some New Testament Invitations to Ethnic Reconciliation," *Evangelical Quarterly* 75, no. 3 (July 2003): 195-213, here 195-202.

[30]Some take these other sheep in 10:16 as Diaspora Jews (John A. T. Robinson, "The Destination and Purpose of St. John's Gospel," *New Testament 6, no. 2 [Jan. 1960]*: 117-31, here 127-28; J. Louis Martyn, "Glimpses into the History of the Johannine Community," 149-76 in *L'Évangile de Jean: Sources, rédaction, théologie* [ed. M. De Jonge; Bibliotheca Ephemeridum Theologicarum Lovaniensium 45; Gembloux: J. Duculot; Leuven: University Press, 1977], 174) or Samaritans (cf. John Bowman, "Samaritan Studies," *Bulletin of the John Rylands Library* 40, no. 2 [1958]: 298-327; Edwin D. Freed, "Samaritan Influence in the Gospel of John," *Catholic Biblical Quarterly* 30, no. 4 [Oct. 1968]: 580-87; Charles H. H. Scobie, "The Origins and Development of Samaritan Christianity," *New Testament Studies* 19, no. 4 [July 1973]: 390-414, here 407), but most see them as Gentile believers (e.g., J. H. Bernard, *A Critical and Exegetical Commentary on the Gospel According to St. John* [2 vols.; ICC; Edinburgh: T. & T. Clark, 1928], 2:361; J. Ramsey Michaels, *John* [Good News Commentaries; San Francisco: Harper & Row, Publishers, 1984], 169). Against some, normal usage suggests that "Greeks" (7:35; 12:20) are Gentiles (discussion in Keener, *John*, 721).

The Breath of Life

What is the significance of Jesus breathing on them? Most scholars see an allusion to Genesis 2:7. As God breathed into the first human the breath of life, so now Jesus imparts new life to his followers.[31] Greek and Hebrew could employ terms for "breath" or "wind" for God's Spirit. Jesus earlier depicted eternal life initiated by the new birth not only in terms of water, but also in terms of wind (3:8), perhaps evoking the resurrection life of God's breath or Spirit in Ezekiel 37:9-14.[32] (That is, as John 3:5-6 probably alludes to Ezekiel 36:25-27, so John 3:8 probably alludes to Ezekiel 37.) It is God's breath that brings life to the new creation, as it did to the old.

---

[31]E.g., Ernst Haenchen, A Commentary on the Gospel of John (2 vols.; trans. Robert W. Funk; ed. Robert W. Funk with Ulrich Busse; Hermeneia; Philadelphia: Fortress, 1984), 2:211; J. N. Sanders, *A Commentary on the Gospel According to St. John* (ed. B. A. Mastin; HNTC; New York: Harper & Row, Publishers, 1968), 433; Max Turner, *The Holy Spirit and Spiritual Gifts in the New Testament Church and Today* (rev. ed.; Peabody, MA: Hendrickson, 1998), 90-92; Keener, *John*, 1204-5; James D. G. Dunn, "Spirit. NT," 3:693-707 in *The New International Dictionary of New Testament Theology* (ed. Colin Brown; Grand Rapids: Zondervan, 1978), 703; Peter F. Ellis, *The Genius of John: A Composition-Critical Commentary on the Fourth Gospel* (Collegeville, MN: Liturgical, 1984), 293; M. Wojciechowski, "Le Don de L'Esprit Saint dans Jean 20.22 selon Tg. Gn. 2.7," *New Testament Studies* 33, no. 2 (1987): 289-92 (though reading too much from the Targumim, which is then used to connect John 20 with Pentecost); Gail R. O'Day, "The Gospel of John: Introduction, Commentary, and Reflections," 9:491-865 in *The New Interpreter's Bible* (12 vols.; ed. Leander E. Keck; Nashville: Abingdon, 1995), 846; Jan A. du Rand, "'n Ellips skeppingsgebeure in die Evangelieverhaal volgens Johannes," *Skrif en Kerk* 21, no. 2 (2000): 243-59. For imagery of a new creation, e.g., Cook, "Exegesis," 8; John P. Meier, "John 20:19-23," *Mid-Stream* 35, no. 4 (1996): 395-98.

[32]Cf. e.g., Max-Alain Chevallier, *Ancien Testament, Hellénisme et Judaïsme, La tradition synoptique, L'oeuvre de Luc* (vol. 1 in *Souffle de Dieu: le Saint-Esprit dans le Nouveau Testament*; Le Point Théologique 26; Paris: Éditions Beauchesne, 1978), 23; D. W. B. Robinson, "Born of Water and Spirit: Does John 3:5 Refer to Baptism?" *The Reformed Theological Review* 25, no. 1 (Jan. 1966): 15-23, here 17.

As a matter of interest, we may pause to ask (as scholars often do) about the relationship between this passage and Pentecost in Acts 2.[33] Some scholars see this passage as a lesser Pentecost, while others see it as John's replacement for or equivalent to Luke's Pentecost. Perhaps on the historical level, we may think of these two events as two levels of impartation, as some scholars argue. On the theological level, however, this is the passage that ties together Jesus's various promises surrounding the Spirit earlier in the Fourth Gospel—Jesus coming to them (14:18), resurrection life (14:19), joy (15:11; 20:20), peace (14:27; 20:21), the Spirit's new birth and indwelling (3:5; 14:17; 20:22), and being sent as witnesses (15:26-27; 20:21). John is not continuing his narrative as late chronologically as Pentecost. At least on the narrative level, this passage must carry the symbolic weight of John's entire theology of the Spirit. What then is his theology of the Holy Spirit?

The Spirit of Purification

First, the Spirit purifies God's people and in a manner that mere ceremonial washings cannot. The image of Jesus breathing new life into his followers in chapter 20 indicates that this emphasis in John's theology of the Spirit continues here. Some ancient Jewish sources (especially among the Essenes) recognized in Ezekiel 36:25-26 that at

---

[33]See discussion (from various perspectives) in e.g., Robert P. Menzies, "John's Place in the Development of Early Christian Pneumatology," 41-52 in *The Spirit and Spirituality: Essays in Honor of Russell P. Spittler* (ed. Wonsuk Ma and Robert P. Menzies; JPTSup 24; London, New York: T&T Clark International, 2004); Keener, *John*, 1196-1200; Turner, *Gifts*, 94-97; idem, "The Concept of Receiving the Spirit in John's Gospel," *VE* 10 (1976): 24-42; Max-Alain Chevallier, "'Pentecôtes' lucaniennes et 'Pentecôtes' johanniques," *RSR* 69, no. 2 (Apr. 1981): 301-13; Donald A. Carson, *The Gospel According to John* (Leicester, England: Inter-Varsity; Grand Rapids: Eerdmans, 1991), 648-55; Joost van Rossum, "The 'Johannine Pentecost': John 20:22 in Modern Exegesis and in Orthodox Theology," *SVTQ* 35, nos 2-3 (1991): 149-67; Philippe H. Menoud, "La Pentecôte lucanienne et l'histoire," *RHPR* 42, nos 2-3 (1962): 141-47; Stanley M. Horton, *What the Bible Says About the Holy Spirit* (Springfield, MO: Gospel Publishing House, 1976), 127-33; W. Bartlett, "The Coming of the Holy Ghost according to the Fourth Gospel," *ExpT* 37 (1925-26): 72-75, here 73; Francis Wright Beare, "The Risen Jesus Bestows the Spirit: A Study of John 20:19-23," *CJT* 4, no. 2 (Apr. 1958): 95-100, here 96; Burge, *Community*, 148.

the end-time the Spirit would purify God's people morally.[34] John develops this emphasis especially through an ongoing contrast with merely natural water, often that used for ritual purification.

The contrast appears regularly in John's Gospel (especially in what is often called its "signs section"). Jesus's baptism in the Spirit is greater than John the Baptist's baptism in water (1:31, 33). Jesus disregards the ritual consecration of six waterpots when he turns water in them into wine (2:6-10).[35]   Whereas some Jewish people may have expected Gentile converts to become like newborn babies after being immersed in water,[36] Jesus summons Nicodemus to a true proselyte baptism in the water of the Spirit (3:5).[37]

In 4:14, Jesus offers "living water"[38] that's greater than the water of Jacob's well, a site holy to the Samaritans. In fact, John's geographic interest is not in holy -sites, such as Jerusalem's temple or the

[34]See 1QS 3.7; 4.21; 1QH 8.30; 16; 4Q255 frg. 2.1; 4Q257 3.10; Craig S. Keener, "The Function of Johannine Pneumatology in the Context of Late First-Century Judaism" (Ph.D. dissertation, New Testament and Christian Origins, Duke University, 1991), 65-69; idem, *The Spirit in the Gospels and Acts: Divine Purity and Power* (Peabody: Hendrickson, 1997), 146-51, 162; F. F. Bruce, "Holy Spirit in the Qumran Texts," *ALUOS* 6 (1966): 49-55, here 52-54; J. Coppens, "Le Don de l'Esprit d'après les textes de Qumrân et le Quatrième Évangile," 209-23 in *L'Évangile de Jean: Études et Problèmes* (Recherches Bibliques 3; Louvain: Desclée de Brouwer, 1958), 211-12, 222; Émile Puech, "L'Esprit saint à Qumrân," *SBFLA* 49 (1999): 283-97; George Johnston, "'Spirit' and 'Holy Spirit' in the Qumran Literature," 27-42 in *New Testament Sidelights: Essays in honor of Alexander Converse Purdy* (ed. Harvey K. McArthur; Hartford: Hartford Seminary Foundation, 1960), 40; Max-Alain Chevallier, "Le souffle de Dieu dans le Judaïsme, aux abords de l'ère chrétienne," *FoiVie* 80, no. 1 (Jan. 1981): 33-46, here 40.

[35]See discussion in Keener, *John*, 509-13.

[36]Later rabbis' association of conversion with becoming like a new child is often noted, e.g., H. W. Watkins, *The Gospel According to John* (ed. Charles John Ellicott; 2nd ed.; Grand Rapids: Zondervan, 1957), 74; Bruce J. Malina and Richard L. Rohrbaugh, *Social-Science Commentary on the Gospel of John* (Minneapolis: Fortress, 1998), 82 (citing *b. Yeb.* 22a; 48b; 62a; 97b; *Bek.* 47a). This view is at least as early as the seventeenth century; see John Lightfoot, *A Commentary on the New Testament from the Talmud and Hebraica* (4 vols.; n.p.: Oxford, 1959; Grand Rapids: Baker, 1979), 3:265.

[37]See discussion more extensively in Keener, *John*, 537-55, esp. 546-50; cf. John Calvin, *Commentary on the Gospel According to John* (2 vols.; trans. William Pringle; Edinburgh: Calvin Translation Society, 1847), 1:111.

[38]A wordplay; "living" water was flowing water, the kind one would get from a spring (cf. e.g., LXX Gen 26:19; Lev 14:5-6, 50-52). But John also thinks of the "water of life" (Rev 7:17; 21:6; 22:1, 17); cf. Ps 36:9; Jer 2:13; 17:13; Oscar Cullmann, *Early Christian Worship* (Philadelphia: Westminster; London: SCM, 1953), 81; Birger Olsson, *Structure and Meaning in the Fourth Gospel: A Text Linguistic Analysis of John 2:1-11 and 4:1-42* (trans. Jean Gray; Lund, Sweden: CWK Gleerup, 1974), 213; Brown, *John*, 1:cxxxv.

Samaritans' Mount Gerizim, but rather the proper sphere of worship, namely in the Spirit of truth (4:20-24).[39] In 5:1-9, the water of a pool associated with healings leaves a man infirm, but Jesus heals him; in 9:1-7 another man is healed in connection with a sacred pool, but only because Jesus sends him there.[40] Jesus himself later takes the role of a servant as he washes his disciples' feet in a scene interspersed with announcement of the coming betrayal (Jn 13).[41]

The key text with reference to John's water motif (key because it offers an explicit explanation) is 7:37-39, where Jesus, on the last day of the Festival of Tabernacles, promises "rivers of living water" (7:2, 37). On this last day of the festival, priests poured water from the Pool of Siloam at the base of the altar to symbolize an expectation stemming from Ezekiel 47 and Zechariah 14. Priests read these passages on the same day. Both of these texts spoke of rivers of living water flowing from the temple and from Jerusalem in the eschatological time.[42] Thus, on the day that they were being read, Jesus announces to the people, "Whoever thirsts, let them come to me; let them drink, whoever believes in me. As the Scripture has said, 'From his belly will flow

---

[39]See discussion more fully in Keener, *John*, 611-19.

[40]Scholars often note the contrast between the two passages; see especially R. Alan Culpepper, *Anatomy of the Fourth Gospel: A Study in Literary Design* (Philadelphia: Fortress, 1983), 139; cf. also Jeffrey L. Staley, "Stumbling in the Dark, Reaching for the Light: Reading Character in John 5 and 9," *Semeia* 53 (1991): 55-80; Dorothy A. Lee, *The Symbolic Narratives of the Fourth Gospel: The Interplay of Form and Meaning* (JSNTSup 95; Sheffield: Sheffield Academic Press, 1994), 105-6; Raymond F. Collins, *These Things Have Been Written: Studies on the Fourth Gospel* (Louvain Theological & Pastoral Monographs 2; Louvain: Peeters; Grand Rapids: Eerdmans, 1990), 23; Rainer Metzner, "Der Geheilte von Johannes 5—Repräsentant des Unglaubens," *ZNW* 90, nos 3-4 (1999): 177-93.

[41]For the footwashing, see especially John Christopher Thomas, *Footwashing in John 13 and the Johannine Community* (JSNTSup 61; Sheffield: JSOT Press, Sheffield Academic, 1991).

[42]See e.g., *t. Suk.* 3:3-10, 18. Among commentators, cf. e.g., C. H. Dodd, *The Interpretation of the Fourth Gospel* (Cambridge: Cambridge University Press, 1965), 350; Archibald M. Hunter, *The Gospel According to John* (Cambridge Bible Commentary; Cambridge: Cambridge University Press, 1965), 84-85; Rudolf Schnackenburg, *The Gospel According to St. John* (3 vols.; trans. Kevin Smyth and J. Massingberd Ford; New York: Herder & Herder, 1968; New York: Seabury, 1980-1982), 2:155; see fuller discussion in Keener, *John*, 722-30 (esp. 725-27).

rivers of living water.'"[43] Jewish people thought of Jerusalem as the "navel" of the earth,[44] but Jesus here depicts himself as the foundation of God's new temple, the source of living water.[45] John explains that once Jesus would be glorified, those who believe in him would receive from him this living water—the Spirit (7:39).

Lest we forget his point, John also takes time to narrate an event at the crucifixion not included in the other extant Gospels. When the soldier pierced Jesus's side with his spear, not only blood but also water came forth (19:34). Historically, the spear may have punctured the pericardial sac around the heart, releasing a watery substance along with the blood.[46] But why does John bother to record this event and even underline it emphatically by noting that he was an eyewitness

---

[43]Scholars differ on the precise syntax here, some seeing water from the believer (Gordon D. Fee, "Once More—John 7:37-39," *Expository Times* 89, no. 4 [Jan. 1978]: 116-18; Joseph Blenkinsopp, "John VII.37-9: Another Note on a Notorious Crux," *New Testament Studies* 6, no. 1 [Oct. 1959]: 95-98; Zane C. Hodges, "Rivers of Living Water: John 7:37-39: Part 7 of Problem Passages in the Gospel of John," *Bibliotheca Sacra* 136, no. 543 [July 1979]: 239-48; Bernard, *John*, 1:282; Juan B. Cortés, "Yet Another Look at Jn 7,37-38," *CBQ* 29, no. 1 [Jan. 1967]: 75-86) and some from Jesus (Dodd, *Interpretation*, 349; Brown, *John*, 1:321-23; James D. G. Dunn, *Baptism in the Holy Spirit: A Re-examination of the New Testament Teaching on the Gift of the Spirit in relation to Pentecostalism Today* [Studies in Biblical Theology, 2nd ser., 15; London: SCM, 1970], 179-80; J. Ramsey Michaels, "The Temple Discourse in John," 200-213 in *New Dimensions in New Testament Study* [ed. Richard N. Longenecker and Merrill C. Tenney; Grand Rapids: Zondervan, 1974], 208-9; M. J. J. Menken, "The Origin of the Old Testament Quotation in John 7:38," *Novum Testamentum* 38, no. 2 [1996]: 160-75; D. Moody Smith, *John* [Abingdon New Testament Commentaries; Nashville: Abingdon, 1999], 174). For our purposes here, it may suffice to note that whether the rivers flow from the believer *or* Jesus, Jesus is the explicit *ultimate* source in 7:39.

[44]See e.g., *Jub.* 8:12; *Sib. Or.* 5:249-50; *b. Yoma* 54b. Cf. also James M. Scott, "Luke's Geographical Horizon," 483-544 in *The Book of Acts in Its Graeco-Roman Setting* (ed. David W. J. Gill and Conrad Gempf; vol. 2 in *The Book of Acts in its First-Century Setting*, 6 vols.; Grand Rapids: Eerdmans; Carlisle: Paternoster, 1994), 526; Philip S. Alexander, "Notes on the 'Imago Mundi' of the Book of Jubilees," *Journal of Jewish Studies* 33, nos 1-2 (1982): 197-213; Mieczyslaw Celestyn Paczkowski, "Gerusalemme – 'ombelico del mondo' nella tradizione cristiana antica." *SBFLA* 55 (2005): 165-202." Greeks applied the label to Delphi (e.g., Euripides *Med.* 667-68; *Orest.* 591; Pindar *Pyth.* 4.74; 8.59-60; 11.10).

[45]Cf. e.g., Lloyd Gaston, *No Stone On Another: Studies in the Significance of the Fall of Jerusalem in the Synoptic Gospels* (NovTSup 23; Leiden: E. J. Brill, 1970), 211; S. H. Hooke, "'The Spirit was not yet,'" *New Testament Studies* 9, no. 4 (July 1963): 372-80, here 377-78; Mary L. Coloe, *God Dwells with Us: Temple Symbolism in the Fourth Gospel* (Collegeville, MN: Liturgical, A Michael Glazier Book, 2001), 132-33.

[46]John Wilkinson, "The Incident of the Blood and Water in John 19.34," *Scottish Journal of Theology* 28, no. 2 (1975): 149-72.

(19:35)?[47] I suspect he does so because it forms a climactic illustration of Jesus's point.[48]   Lifted up and glorified, crowned king of the Jews, Jesus by his death provided living water for his people. The Book of Revelation expresses John's point well—"Let the one who thirsts come and drink freely from the water of the river of life" (Rev 22:17). John's Gospel deals with the water of the Spirit, of which traditional ritual purification is at best a szymbol.

The Spirit of Prophetic Empowerment

Second, and of primary importance for our discussion of John's missiology, the Spirit involves prophetic power. Whereas some Jewish texts stressed the Spirit's purifying role, most stressed the Spirit's prophetic role.[49] Jesus's closing discourses to his disciples emphasized this aspect of the Spirit's work, including comments about sending the Spirit. The Father sends the Spirit in Jesus's name both to teach them and to help them recall his teachings (14:26). Likewise, Jesus sends the Spirit to bear witness concerning him (15:26), which the disciples will also do (15:27).

The prophets of old both heard God and proclaimed what they heard, and we find both elements in this Gospel. In 10:3-5, 16, 27, Jesus

---

[47]Although many scholars challenge this position, I have argued for the identity of the beloved disciple with the author, and that of both with the apostle John, in Keener, *John*, 81-139.

[48]John selects for inclusion what he does to communicate a point (Jn 20:30-31). See e.g., Matthew Vellanickal, "Blood and Water," *Jeevadhara* 8, no. 45 (1978): 218-30; James McPolin, *John* (New Testament Message 6; Wilmington, DE: Michael Glazier, 1979), 249; Raymond E. Brown, *The Death of the Messiah: From Gethsemane to Grave. A Commentary on the Passion Narratives in the Four Gospels* (2 vols.; New York: Doubleday, 1994), 1178-82; Craig R. Koester, *Symbolism in the Fourth Gospel: Meaning, Mystery, Community* (Minneapolis: Fortress, 1995), 181. Others find an allusion to water from the wilderness rock (e.g., T. Francis Glasson, *Moses in the Fourth Gospel* [Naperville, IL: Alec R. Allenson, 1963], 52-53, citing church fathers).

[49]See e.g., Robert P. Menzies, *Empowered for Witness: The Spirit in Luke-Acts* (London, New York: T & T Clark International, 2004), 49-101; idem, *The Development of Early Christian Pneumatology with special reference to Luke-Acts* (JSNTSup 54; Sheffield: Sheffield Academic Press, 1991), 53-112; idem, "Spirit and Power in Luke-Acts: A Response to Max Turner," *JSNT* 49 (1993): 11-20; Max Turner, *Power from on High: The Spirit in Israel's Restoration and Witness in Luke-Acts* (Sheffield: Sheffield Academic Press, 1996), 86-104; Youngmo Cho, *Spirit and Kingdom in the Writings of Luke and Paul: An Attempt to Reconcile these Concepts* (foreword by R. P. Menzies; Paternoster Biblical Monographs; Waynesboro, GA; Milton Keynes, UK: Paternoster, 2005), 10-51; Keener, "Pneumatology," 69-77; idem, *Spirit*, 10-13, 31-33.

talks about his sheep (true disciples) hearing his voice; and they "know" him[50] just as the Father knows him and he knows the Father (10:14-15). This bespeaks of the depth of relationship with Jesus that God has made available to us, the context for this being the following incident recorded in chapter 9:

A blind man healed by Jesus becomes his follower and, as a consequence, is expelled from the synagogue by Israel's supposed 'guardians'. Jesus compares these hostile guardians to strangers, thieves, and wolves who exploit the sheep (10:1, 5, 8, 10, 12); they resemble the false shepherds of Israel in Ezekiel 34:2-10. By contrast, Jesus is the "good shepherd" (10:11, 14), who would lay down his life for the sheep to protect them from the thieves. Jesus is using biblical imagery—the chief shepherd of Israel in the Hebrew scriptures was God (Ezek 34:11-16), whose role Jesus appropriately fills here. Meanwhile, this formerly blind man, although now excluded from Israel's religious community by its leaders, is embraced by Jesus as truly one of God's people, who were often compared with God's sheep in Scripture (e.g., Ps 100:3; Ezek 34:2). This man, who heeded Jesus, becomes an example of the sheep who heed his voice, which Israel failed to do (Ps 95:7-11).[51] Jesus's disciples are another example of those hearing his voice. He called them "friends" because whatever he heard from the Father he shared with them (15:15).[52]

John is very clear that hearing Jesus's voice is an experience that should continue among the community of believers.[53] Just as he did not speak from himself (12:49; 14:10), neither would the Spirit speak from

---

[50]OT language for Israel's covenant relationship with God (e.g., Exod 6:7; in the new covenant, Jer 24:7; 31:33-34).

[51]Most Johannine scholars today also view him as a model for John's primary audience; e.g., J. Louis Martyn, *History and Theology in the Fourth Gospel* (Nashville: Abingdon, 1968), 40; Severino Pancaro, *The Law in the Fourth Gospel* (Leiden: E. J. Brill, 1975), 247-52; David Rensberger, *Johannine Faith and Liberating Community* (Philadelphia: Westminster, 1988), 42.

[52]Sharing rather than keeping secrets was one key element in ancient Mediterranean ideologies of friendship; see discussion in Keener, *John*, 1010; idem, "Friendship," 380-88 in *Dictionary of New Testament Background* (ed. Craig A. Evans and Stanley Porter; Downers Grove, IL: InterVarsity, 2000), 383.

[53]On Johannine knowledge of God, see e.g., Keener, *John*, 234-47 (esp. 243-47); idem, "Studies in the Knowledge of God in the Fourth Gospel in Light of Its Historical Context" (M.Div. Thesis, The Assemblies of God Theological Seminary, 1986).

himself (16:13).[54] And just as Jesus told his "friends" that whatever he heard from the Father he would tell them, he explains now that whatever the Spirit hears from him, the Spirit will speak to them (16:13). Further, just as Jesus came to glorify not himself but the Father, the Spirit comes to reveal and glorify Jesus (16:13-15).[55] This means that disciples today at least potentially are able to hear Jesus as clearly as did the first disciples, except now with the advantage of a retrospective understanding of Jesus's identity and mission.[56]

Likewise, disciples who hear from Jesus will also reveal him to the world, in connection with the Spirit (15:26-27).[57] Whereas the Father sent Jesus into the world and Jesus sends the disciples into the world (17:18), John does not tell us that the Spirit is sent to the world. Rather, Jesus says, "If I go, I will send Him to you" (16:7; cf. 15:26).[58] After Jesus promises to send the advocate to them, he says that the Spirit will "convict" the world (16:8). In a context where the Spirit comes as witness (15:26) and perhaps as advocate (one possible translation for *paraklētos* in 14:16, 26; 15:26; and 16:7), we might render the Spirit's activity here as "prosecuting" the world.[59] He will "charge" the world regarding sin, righteousness, and judgment. These were activities of Jesus earlier in the Gospel (3:20; 8:46), and the particulars offered in 16:8-10 also involve his person or acts. The point appears to be that Jesus, who confronted the world in this Gospel, will continue to confront it, because his presence remains. Now, however, that presence is revealed through the Spirit's ministry in and through the life and message of disciples.

---

[54]I.e., not on his own authority, e.g., *T. Ab.* 15:8; 19:4A; Philostratus *Hrk.* 8.2.

[55]Cf. Heinrich Schlier, "Zum Begriff des Geistes nach dem Johannesevangelium," 264-271 in *Besinnung auf das Neue Testament* (Exegetische Aufsätze und Vorträge II; Freiburg: Herder, 1964), 269: the Spirit illumines the work of Jesus in his glory.

[56]I discuss this more fully and in more explicitly practical terms in my *Gift & Giver: The Holy Spirit for Today* (Grand Rapids: Baker, 2001), 39-42.

[57]Although the passage involves the first disciples who were with him "from the beginning" (cf. 2:11; 8:25; 16:4; Acts 1:21-22), but John expects his audience to understand their own experience analogously (1 Jn 2:24; 3:11; 2 Jn 6).

[58]Cf. Henry Efferin, "The Paraclete in John 14-16," *Stulos Theological Journal* 1, no. 2 (1993): 149-56; earlier, Luther *Sermon on Jn 16*.

[59]With e.g., C. K. Barrett, *The Gospel According to St. John: An Introduction with Commentary and Notes on the Greek Text* (2nd ed.; Philadelphia: Westminster, 1978), 90; O'Day, "John," 771; argued in Keener, *John*, 1030-35.

The Spirit and God's Presence

The Spirit empowers us to communicate Jesus to others because, through the Spirit, Jesus's presence remains in our midst. He sends the advocate so that "He may be with you forever" (14:16), and be "in you" (14:17); thus, the Father and Son make their "dwelling place" within us (14:23). In fact, even Jesus's promise of many dwelling places in the Father's house apparently communicates the same point. Against the common assumption that the Father's house (as used here) must mean heaven,[60] its other uses in the Gospel refer to a father's household (8:35) or to the temple (2:16-17). Thus, only context can specify what it means here.[61] Most essentially, we may surmise that it will involve the place of the Father's presence.

What does Jesus mean by dwelling places (or "rooms" in some translations) that he prepares in the Father's house in 14:2? This Greek term, *monē*, appears in only one other location in the entire New Testament—John 14:23,[62] which is in this same context and deliberately clarifies its use here. In that passage, Jesus declares that he and the Father will come and make their dwelling place (*monē*) within believers.[63] The cognate verb is frequent in the context, referring to the Spirit or Jesus's message dwelling or remaining in believers, or believers dwelling or remaining in Christ (14:17; 15:4-10, 16).[64]

---

[60]Though argued only rarely by scholars, e.g., Holwerda, *Spirit*, 20, n. 52; also Calvin, *John*, 2:81.

[61]Many see an allusion to the temple; e.g., H. Leonard Pass, *The Glory of the Father: A Study in S. John XIII-XVII* (London: A. R. Mowbray & Company, 1935), 66-68; G. H. C. MacGregor, *The Gospel of John* (MNTC; London: Hodder & Stoughton, 1928), 305.

[62]It appears only once in the Apostolic Fathers (in Papias), twice in Josephus (*Ant.* 8.350; 13.41); and never, so far as I can tell, in the LXX (though 15 times in the Philonic corpus).

[63]Many recognize a connection between the two uses in this context; see Robert Alan Berg, "Pneumatology and the History of the Johannine community: Insights from the Farewell Discourses and the First Epistle" (Ph.D. dissertation, Graduate School of Drew University, 1988; Ann Arbor, MI: University Microfilms International, 1989), 107-10.

[64]This is a favorite verb for John, though not always carrying its full theological import; it appear 40 times in the Gospel, which is about 33.9% of NT uses, though John is just 11% of the NT text (i.e., over three times the NT average). The Johannine epistles employ the verb 27 times, or 22.9% of NT uses, or 13.7 times (1370% more) than average. Together the Gospel and epistles offer about 56.8% of NT examples of this verb.

What does Jesus mean in this context by, "I will come again to you" (14:3)? Later, his coming (14:18) is associated with the giving of the Spirit (14:16-17) and resurrection life (14:19). But it also involves Jesus and the Father coming to the believer and making their dwelling place there (14:23). In contrast to his second coming, the disciples would see him but the world would not (14:19). Again in a context emphasizing the coming of the Spirit (16:13-15), Jesus says he would return to reveal himself to them, the context clearly meaning after his death and resurrection (16:17-22). Jesus refers here not to his coming at the end of the age[65] but to his coming to inaugurate eschatological life in the lives of his disciples (20:19-23).

Jesus repeatedly says, "I am going . . . " (14:2-5, 28; 16:5, 7), referring in most of these texts to going to the Father by way of death (8:22; 13:33, 36; 16:28; cf. 16:20-22).[66] He tells his disciples that they know where he is going and the way he will get there (14:4); but Thomas protests that they know neither the where nor the way (14:5). The first disciples did not understand 14:2-3 by itself any better than we understand these verses isolated from Jesus's following explanation, which was that he is going to the Father and that he himself is the way (14:6). He is not telling the disciples that at his second coming they are going with him to the dwelling place prepared for them. Rather he declares that those who come to the Father through him—i.e., those who believe and abide in Jesus—are in the Father's presence.[67]

That is to say (regarding 20:19-23), Jesus's coming to give his disciples the Spirit inaugurates his presence in their lives in a new dimension. Now we can do God's work because God's Spirit lives in us.

---

[65]Though not at 14:2-3, I do acknowledge future eschatology in John's Gospel (see e.g., Jn 5:28-29; 6:39-40, 44, 54; 12:48; with many, e.g., Werner Georg Kümmel, *The Theology of the New Testament According to its Major Witnesses—Jesus, Paul, John* [trans. John E. Steely; Nashville: Abingdon, 1973], 294-95; Barrett, *John*, 68-69; Burge, *Community*, 115). Bultmann's forced-choice logic that requires him to excise such passages as secondary ignores the coexistence of realized and future eschatology in the Qumran scrolls or, for that matter, Jesus's teachings and Paul's letters.

[66]Some texts admittedly look beyond the death and resurrection to Jesus's longer-range presence with the Father away from the disciples (14:12; 16:10); John's love for riddles and wordplays leaves considerable ambiguity, probably deliberately.

[67]On Jesus as the "way" to the Father's presence here, see e.g., Robert H. Gundry, "'In my Father's House are many Monai' (Joh 14:2)," *Zeitschrift für die Neutestamentliche Wissenschaft* 58 (1967): 68-72, here 70.

"I Send You" (20:21)

Jesus sends the disciples into the world just as the Father sent him into the world (17:18). Some may object that such passages apply only to the first disciples in John's narrative world. This objection, however, misunderstands the function of his narrative.[68] Just as John the Baptist functions as a paradigmatic witness in the opening of John's Gospel,[69] so do Jesus's disciples function as paradigmatic for the community of believers. John is interested in those who believe through their proclamation (17:20). It is not only the first disciples that are fruit-bearing branches on Jesus the vine (15:1-8) who must abide and bear fruit (15:2-5, 8), persevere (15:6), and love one another (15:12). In his epistles, John does not limit the Spirit to the Twelve (who received the promises of the advocate in chapters 14-16); rather, he makes clear that those promises are for all true believers (1 Jn 2:20, 27; 3:24; 4:2, 13).[70] Not all believers in the community have the same role as the first disciples, but the community as a whole shares their same mission and purpose—i.e., to make Christ known.

Christological Confessions

A central part of this mission is to proclaim Jesus's identity. In John's Gospel, among the models of preaching Jesus already noted are Philip and the Samaritan woman. Yet John himself offers us a model by how he himself, inspired by the Spirit, preaches Jesus. One may

---

[68]For broader applicability of Johannine promises of the Spirit, cf. e.g., Beare, "Spirit"; D. Moody Smith, "John 16:1-15," *Interpretation* 33 (1, Jan. 1979): 58-62, here 60; George Eldon Ladd, *A Theology of the New Testament* (Grand Rapids: Eerdmans, 1974), 220, 268, 296; James Montgomery Boice, Witness and Revelation in the Gospel of John (Grand Rapids: Zondervan, 1970; Exeter: Paternoster Press, n.d.), 143-44; Horton, *Spirit*, 120-21.

[69]Cf. Hooker, "Baptist," 358; Boice, Witness, 26; Walter Wink, *John the Baptist in the Gospel Tradition* (Cambridge: Cambridge University, 1968), 105; Collins, *Written*, 8-11; Harrison, "John 1:14," 25; Mathias Rissi, "Jn 1:1-18 (The Eternal Word)," *Interpretation* 31 (1977): 394-401, here 398; C. H. Dodd, *Historical Tradition in the Fourth Gospel* (Cambridge: Cambridge University, 1965), 299.

[70]Indeed, 1 Jn 2:27 may deliberately echo Jn 14:26 (with Dunn, *Baptism*, 197).

compare the following various christological confessions he records in the Gospel:[71]

- John the Baptist calls Jesus the "Lamb of God who takes away the sin of the world!" (1:29).[72]
- Nathanael declares, "Rabbi, You are God's Son! You are the king of Israel!" (1:49)
- The Samaritans acknowledge, "This one is truly the world's savior!" (4:42).
- Peter confesses, "You are God's holy one!" (6:69).[73]
- Thomas makes this climactic confession of faith—"My Lord and my God!" (20:28).

Jesus affirms as true Thomas' confession, yet he praises those who can have such faith without a resurrection appearance (20:29). It is here that John explains this is why he wrote his Gospel—so those who have not seen may nevertheless believe Jesus's identity (20:30-31).

Let us add to these confessions in John Gospel Jesus's own declarations of his identity:

- "I am the bread of life" (6:35, 41, 48, 51) to sustain us.
- "I am the light of the world" (8:12; 95) to enlighten us.
- "I am the door" (10:7, 9) to welcome us.

---

[71]These confessions need not all progress from lesser to greater (M. Baron, "La progression des confessions de foi dans les dialogues de saint Jean," *Bible et Vie Chrétienne* 82 [1968]: 32-44), though 20:28 is certainly the climactic one.

[72]The background probably involves the sacrificial lamb, with Schnackenburg, *John*, 1:299; G. Ashby, "The Lamb of God—II," *Journal of Theology for Southern Africa* 25 (1978): 62-65; Bruce H. Grigsby, "The Cross as an Expiatory Sacrifice in the Fourth Gospel," *Journal for the Study of the New Testament* 15 (1982): 51-80; Lightfoot, *Gospel*, 97; Craig Keener, "Lamb," 641-42 in *Dictionary of the Later New Testament & Its Developments* (ed. Ralph P. Martin and Peter H. Davids; Downers Grove, IL: InterVarsity Press, 1997), 641. This might be combined with the servant in Isa 53:7; so Schnackenburg, *John*, 1:300; Brown, *John*, 1:60-63; George L. Carey, "The Lamb of God and Atonement Theories," *Tyndale Bulletin* 32 (1981): 97-122. Cf. also the sacrificial lamb of Exod 29:38-46, in Enz, "Exodus," 214.

[73]The probable reading here, with e.g., Bernard, *John*, 1:223; Bruce M. Metzger, *A Textual Commentary on the Greek New Testament* (London, New York: United Bible Societies, 1971), 215. Against some scribes' attempts to harmonize readings, John supplies a variety of christological confessions.

- "I am the good shepherd" (10:11, 14) to protect and care for us.
- "I am the resurrection and the life" (11:25) to raise us.
- "I am the way and the truth and the life" (14:6) to bring us to the Father.
- "I am the true vine" (15:1) to nourish us with continuous life.
- "I am" (8:58)—the greatest declaration of all—as the God of the patriarchs and prophets.[74]

Such declarations are a fitting focus for a Gospel whose prologue is framed by confessions of Jesus's deity (1:1, 18).[75]   Indeed, so is the body of John's Gospel if we connect the prologue's claim with Thomas' confession in 20:28.[76] Ancient biographies were supposed to focus on their protagonists;[77] John naturally focuses on Jesus in this Gospel, proclaiming Jesus's identity to his audience "so that you may believe" (20:31) as the Spirit brings the hearers into real encounters with Christ (16:7-15).

Jesus Revealed in the Community's Love

We who are sent to preach Jesus present him not only through our words, but (like Jesus himself) through our works. Believers will do the kinds of works Jesus did (14:10-12), many of which were miraculous signs (5:20; 7:3, 21; 9:3-4; 10:25, 32, 37-38; 15:24). But his

---

[74]Some of these evoke divine or Wisdom images in Scripture or early Judaism, but "I am" is the most explicit (Exod 3:14; Isa 41:4; 43:10; cf. Lightfoot, *Gospel*, 134-35; Hunter, *John*, 89; David Mark Bell, *'I Am' in John's Gospel: Literary Function, Background and Theological Implications* [JSNTSup 124; Sheffield: Sheffield Academic Press, 1996], 258). Priests apparently used these very Isaiah texts during the festival at which Jesus declared, "I am" (Ethelbert Stauffer, *Jesus and His Story* [trans. Richard and Clara Winston; New York: Alfred A. Knopf, 1960], 91).

[75]With Boismard, *Prologue*, 76-77.

[76]Oscar Cullmann, *The Christology of the New Testament* (Philadelphia: Westminster; London: SCM, 1959), 308. I do argue for reading Jn 21 as an original part of the Gospel (Keener, *John*, 1219-22; cf. also Bruce, *John*, 398; Paul S. Minear, "The Original Functions of John 21," *Journal of Biblical Literature* 102, no. 1 [1983]: 85-98); my point here is only that it is not part of the main body of the Gospel.

[77]On ancient biographies and the Gospels see especially Richard A. Burridge, *What Are the Gospels? A Comparison with Graeco-Roman Biography* (SNTSMS 70; Cambridge: Cambridge University, 1992); more recently also Craig S. Keener, *Christobiography* (Grand Rapids: Eerdmans, 2019).

"work" also summarizes his entire mission (4:34; 17:4). Presumably John (like Luke and other New Testament writers) does expect continuing miracles among Jesus's followers. However, there is another kind of "sign" John specifies that reveals God's character and light in a dark world. In 15:1-11, Jesus says that disciples, as branches bearing the fruit natural to the vine, should love one another. By loving others we show the world more of God's heart.

In 17:21, Jesus prayed that we his followers would be one so "that the world may believe that you sent me." In 17:23, he went on to pray that we would be perfected in unity so "that the world may know that you sent me and that you loved them even as you loved me." Thus, part of our greatest witness is the supernatural testimony of Jesus's reality by the divine love that believers demonstrate to one another—at least when we are truly depending on and imitating our Lord.

In 13:4-10, assuming the posture of a servant,[78] Jesus washes the disciples' feet, in the context of his impending passion (13:1-3, 11).[79] Although disciples did almost anything for their teachers that servants would do, the one exception was apparently the demeaning work of dealing with the feet (e.g., washing them, carrying sandals).[80] Yet Jesus adopts this servile posture and summons his disciples to follow his example, doing the same for one another (13:12-15). In 13:34-35, he commands us, "Love one another, even as I have loved you. By this, everyone will know that you are my disciples." Jesus titles this injunction a "new commandment," not because it involves love (which was already commanded in Leviticus 19:18),[81] but because of a new standard—that being, "as I have loved you." That is, to love one another as he loves us is to love to the extent that we lay down our lives

---

[78]Cf. Homer *Od.* 19.344-48, 353-60, 376, 388-93, 505; Apollodorus *Epitome* 1.2; Thomas, Footwashing, 40-41, 50-55.

[79]Jesus's act here prefigures the passion (with R. Alan Culpepper, "The Johannine *Hypodeigma*: A Reading of John 13," *Semeia* 53 [1991]: 133-52).

[80]*B. Ket.* 96a, cited by various commentators (cf. W. D. Davies, *The Sermon on the Mount* [Cambridge: Cambridge University, 1966], 135; Leon Morris, *The Gospel According to John: The English Text with Introduction, Exposition and Notes* [NICNT; Grand Rapids: Eerdmans, 1971], 141).

[81]Early Judaism stressed the love commandment (e.g., *Jub.* 36:4, 8; *m. Ab.* 1:12; *Sipra Qed.* pq. 4.200.3.7; Thomas Söding, "Feindeshass und Bruderliebe. Beobachtungen zur essenischen Ethik," *Revue de Qumran* 16 [4, 1995]: 601-19; Reinhard Neudecker, "'And You Shall Love Your Neighbor as Yourself—I Am the Lord' [Lev 19,18] in Jewish Interpretation," *Biblica* 73, no. 4 [1992]: 496-517).

for one another (cf. 1 Jn 3:16). This is the greatest sign of Jesus's reality and character that he has given to his people. The God of grace and truth, who revealed his glory in the cross, makes that message believable to the world when the world sees the church believing and living the heart of God.

Compare John 1:18 ("No one has beheld God at any time; but the only God, who is in the Father's bosom, has made him known") with 1 John 4:12 ("No one has beheld God at any time. If we love one another, God abides in us, and his love is perfected in us"). How will the world see God's heart now? Not only through our words preaching Christ, but also through our lives following his example.

Conclusion

Jesus is the model in this Gospel for what it means to be "sent"— "As the Father sent me, even so I send you." The object of this mission, as in the case of Jesus, must be the world— "For God in this way loved the world." The Spirit, who comes to testify about Jesus, enables this mission by continuing to make him (the Word) present in his followers' word—"Receive the Holy Spirit" entails our empowerment for prophetic witness. Lastly, we as Jesus's followers must present the living Lord both by our words and by our works—i.e., by our witness and by our love.

Our mission is to present Christ in prophetic power, Jesus speaking in us to bring people to experience him for themselves; and to be a community of such divine love that outsiders can see and be drawn to God's heart for the world.

Chapter 3   Power of Pentecost:

Luke's Missiology in

Acts 1-2

I have written a four-volume commentary on Acts,[1] a biblical book that provides more than enough insights by itself for this series on New Testament missiology. The line between writing a missiological commentary on Acts and developing Luke's missiology in Acts would be rather thin, for Acts is about mission. Therefore, I am focusing the discussion on the opening two chapters of Acts, which set the tone for the rest of the book by showing how God's Spirit empowers cross-cultural mission.[2]

The beginning of Acts recapitulates the end of Luke 24,[3] hence functions as the pivot between Luke's Gospel and Acts. It is thus a critical section for showing how the message of his Gospel will apply to the Church. In this introductory section, Acts 1:8 is central—"You

---

[1]Craig Keener, *Acts: An Exegetical Commentary* (4 vols.; Grand Rapids: Baker Academic, 2012-2015); see now also Craig Keener, *Acts* (New Cambridge Bible Commentary; Cambridge: Cambridge University Press, 2020).

[2]These two chapters go beyond the introduction proper (and certainly beyond the preface), but are nevertheless foundational for the rest of Acts (with e.g., Steve Walton, "Where Does the Beginning of Acts End?" 447-67 in *The Unity of Luke-Acts* [ed. Joseph Verheyden; BETL 142; Leuven: Leuven University Press, 1999], esp. 466).

[3]As generally noted, e.g., Rudolf Pesch, *Die Apostelgeschichte* (2 vols.; Evangelisch-KathKomNT 5; Zürich: Benziger Verlag, 1986), 1:61, 72; J. Bradley Chance, *Acts* (SHBC; Macon, GA: Smyth & Helwys, 2007), 34; Denzil R. Miller, *Empowered for Global Mission: A Missionary Look at the Book of Acts* (foreword by John York; N.p.: Life Publishers, 2005), 56-60; M. D. Goulder, *Type and History in Acts* (London: S. P. C. K., 1964), 16-17; Mikeal C. Parsons, *The Departure of Jesus in Luke-Acts: The Ascension Narratives in Context* (JSNTSup 21; Sheffield: JSOT Press, 1987), 189-90. For such recapitulation elsewhere, see e.g., Josephus *Ag. Ap.* 2.1; Chariton *Chaer*. 5.1.1-2; David Edward Aune, *The New Testament in its Literary Environment* (LEC 8; Philadelphia: Westminster, 1987), 90, 117; Daniel Marguerat, *Les Actes des Apôtres (1-12)* (Commentaire du Nouveau Testament, 2nd series, 5 A; Genève: Labor et Fides, 2007), 36.

will be witnesses . . . to the ends of the earth once the Spirit comes on you" (a verse to be examined in more detail later).

In this essay, I will briefly survey the following:

- The *Promise* of Pentecost (1:4-8)
- The *Preparation* for Pentecost (1:12-26)
- The *Proofs* of Pentecost (2:1-4)
- The *Peoples* of Pentecost (2:5-13)
- The *Prophecy* of Pentecost (2:17-21)
- The *Preaching* of Pentecost (2:22-40)
- The *Purpose* of Pentecost (2:41-47)

Thus I will try to survey some elements of various paragraphs in this opening section of Acts, although some of these paragraphs (especially the first one) will require much fuller comment for our purposes than others.

The Promise of Pentecost (1:4-8)

Jesus calls his disciples' attention to a source of power so central that they must remain in Jerusalem and await the Father's promise, rather than attempting to fulfill the mission in their own strength (1:4). Luke here emphasizes that we cannot succeed in Christ's mission without his power. Jesus had already set the example for this dependence in Luke's Gospel (as Acts 10:38 will reiterate).[4]   As introductions in ancient literature often traced the primary themes that a book would address,[5] this introductory paragraph in Acts' opening section is one that must be explored in greater detail.

---

[4]For parallels between the model of Jesus in Luke's Gospel and the church's experience of the Spirit, see e.g., Charles H. Talbert, *Literary Patterns, Theological Themes, and the Genre of Luke-Acts* (SBLMS 20; Missoula, MT: Scholars, 1974), 16; Roger Stronstad, *The Charismatic Theology of St. Luke* (Peabody, MA: Hendrickson, 1984), 51; Robert L. Brawley, *Luke-Acts and the Jews: Conflict, Apology, and Conciliation* (SBLMS 33; Atlanta: Scholars, 1987), 24-25.

[5]See e.g., Polybius 3.1.3 – 3.5.9, esp. 3.1.7; 11.1.4-5; *Rhet. Alex.* 29, 1436a.33-39; Dionysius of Halicarnassus *Thuc.* 19; *Lysias* 24; Cicero *Or. Brut.* 40.137; Virgil *Aen.* 1.1-6; Aulus Gellius pref. 25; Soranus *Gynec.* 1.intro.2; 1.1.3; 2.5.9 [25.78]; Philostratus *Vit. Apoll.* 7.1; 8.1.

Jesus talks to his disciples about the kingdom (1:3) and the Spirit (1:4-5). The Old Testament prophets had already associated the outpouring of the Spirit with the end-time restoration of Israel (e.g., Isa 44:3; 59:21; Ezek 36:26-27; 37:14; 39:29; Joel 2:28-29).[6] The disciples, then, ask the obvious question—Is Jesus about to restore the kingdom? (1:6). He answers that the kingdom will eventually come (1:7), but the Spirit is given now so that they can prepare for its coming by evangelizing the nations (1:8). Because the disciples expected the Spirit eschatologically, they would understand Jesus's promise of the Spirit as involving the coming of the future. Thus, once knowing that the Spirit would precede the consummation of the kingdom, they should understand that he (the Spirit) would be giving them power to live out some of the life of the future kingdom in the present—an idea found in many subsequent New Testament texts (Rom 8:11, 23; 14:17; 1 Cor 2:9-10; 2 Cor 5:5; Gal 5:5; 6:8; Eph 1:13-14; 2 Thess 2:13; Heb 6:4-5).[7]

In Acts 1:8, Jesus promises that the disciples will receive power when the Spirit comes. What does Luke mean by "power?" In his Gospel and Acts narratives, the following verses constitute the most common expressions of that power.

---

[6] The eschatological association of the Spirit is stronger in the prophets than in early Judaism, but cf. Sir 36:14-16; Max-Alain Chevallier, *Souffle de Dieu: le Saint-Esprit dans le Nouveau Testament* (vol. 1: *Ancien Testament, Hellénisme et Judaïsme, La tradition synoptique, L'oeuvre de Luc*; Le Point Théologique 26; Paris: Éditions Beauchesne, 1978), 31-32; Wonsuk Ma, *Until the Spirit Comes: The Spirit of God in the Book of Isaiah* (JSOTSup 271; Sheffield: Sheffield Academic Press, 1999), 175-78, 210-11; W. D. Davies, *Paul and Rabbinic Judaism: Some Rabbinic Elements in Pauline Theology* (4th ed.; Philadelphia: Fortress, 1980), 208-17; Robert P. Menzies, *The Development of Early Christian Pneumatology with special reference to Luke-Acts* (JSNTSup 54; Sheffield: Sheffield Academic Press, 1991), 104-8; idem, *Empowered for Witness: The Spirit in Luke-Acts* (London, New York: T & T Clark International, 2004), 94-98, 232-43.

[7] E.g., the "downpayment" of the Spirit (2 Cor 1:22; 5:5; Eph 1:14); on this meaning, see e.g., Gen 38:17-18, 20 LXX; Oscar Cullmann, *The Early Church* (ed. A. J. B. Higgins; London: SCM, 1956), 117; George Eldon Ladd, *The New Testament and Criticism* (Grand Rapids: Eerdmans, 1967), 91; *New Documents Illustrating Early Christianity: A Review of the Greek Inscriptions and Papyri published in 1976* (vol. 1; ed. G. H. R. Horsley; North Ryde, N.S.W.: The Ancient History Documentary Research Centre, Macquarie University, 1981), 1, §33, p. 83; for first fruits (Rom 8:23), see Neill Q. Hamilton, *The Holy Spirit and Eschatology in Paul* (Scottish Journal of Theology Occasional Papers 6; Edinburgh: Oliver & Boyd, 1957), 19; George Eldon Ladd, *A Theology of the New Testament* (Grand Rapids: Eerdmans, 1974), 370.

- Luke 4:36—Jesus cast out demons with power.
- Luke 5:17—Power was present for healing.
- Luke 6:19—Power was coming from Jesus to heal.
- Luke 8:46—Power came from Jesus to heal.
- Luke 9:1—Jesus gave the Twelve power over demons.
- Acts 3:12—Peter insisted that it was not by his and John's own power or holiness that the man was healed, but by Jesus's name.
- Acts 4:7—The authorities demanded, "By what power, or in what name" the man was healed.
- Acts 6:8—Stephen, "full of grace and power," was doing wonders and signs.[8]
- Acts 10:38—Peter declared that Jesus healed all who were oppressed by the devil because he was anointed with the Spirit and power.

When John Wimber and others spoke of power evangelism, they were echoing this frequent Lukan motif.[9] It should be noted how closely Luke's account connects this empowerment with the Spirit. The Hebrew scriptures often associated the Spirit with prophetic empowerment, among other activities. By the era of the early Church, Jewish sources were apt to focus on this activity even more specifically, as a number of scholars (most extensively Robert Menzies) have

---

[8]A dominant Greek term for "miracles" in the Gospels and Acts is literally "powers"; we should perhaps not read too much into the etymological connection, but Luke might at least play on it (cf. e.g., Luke 10:13; 19:37; Acts 2:22; 8:13; 19:11; see *BDAG*). Paul can also associate "power" with miracles (Rom 15:19), though he more often associates it with the "weak" miracle-working message itself (Rom 1:16; 1 Cor 1:18, 24; 2:4-5; Phil 3:10; 1 Thess 1:5; cf. 2 Tim 1:8). On power's association with the Spirit in Paul, see Gordon D. Fee, *God's Empowering Presence: The Holy Spirit in the Letters of Paul* (Peabody: Hendrickson, 1994), 35-36; Peter J. Gräbe, "*Dunamis* (in the Sense of Power) as a Pneumatological Concept in the Main Pauline Letters," *BZ* 36 (2, 1992): 226-35.

[9]See John Wimber with Kevin Springer, *Power Evangelism* (San Francisco: Harper & Row, Publishers, 1986).

shown.[10] Because the Spirit was so closely associated with prophecy and the kinds of activities undertaken by prophets, Jesus was promising the disciples that the same Spirit who spoke through the prophets would speak through them. If we are too accustomed to that notion to catch its full force, we might imagine Jesus saying to us, "You will be like Isaiah" or "You will be like Jeremiah" or "You will be like Deborah."

Because Luke already noted that Jesus's commission is grounded in scripture (Luke 24:44-46), he invites us to hear echoes of scripture in Jesus's words. The promise that the Spirit would empower them[11] as "witnesses to . . . the ends of the earth" reflects the language of Isaiah.[12] For he spoke of Israel (or its remnant) as being witnesses for YHWH (Isa 43:10; 44:8), a role applied here to witnesses for Jesus. The prophet spoke of God empowering his people through his Spirit in that time (e.g., Isa 32:15; 44:3), including to speak for him (42:1; 48:16; 59:21; 61:1). The "ends of the earth" also echoes Isaiah, especially 49:6, which

---

[10]See e.g., Menzies, *Empowered*, 49-101; idem, *Development*, 53-112; idem, "Spirit and Power in Luke-Acts: A Response to Max Turner," *JSNT* 49 (1993): 11-20; Max Turner, *Power from on High: The Spirit in Israel's Restoration and Witness in Luke-Acts* (Sheffield: Sheffield Academic Press, 1996), 86-104; Youngmo Cho, *Spirit and Kingdom in the Writings of Luke and Paul: An Attempt to Reconcile these Concepts* (foreword by R. P. Menzies; Paternoster Biblical Monographs; Waynesboro, GA; Milton Keynes, UK: Paternoster, 2005), 10-51; Craig S. Keener, "The Function of Johannine Pneumatology in the Context of Late First Century Judaism" (Ph.D. dissertation, Duke University, 1991), 69-77; idem, *The Spirit in the Gospels and Acts: Divine Purity and Power* (Peabody: Hendrickson Publishers, 1997), 10-13, 31-33; in the OT, Christopher J. H. Wright, *Knowing the Holy Spirit through the Old Testament* (Downers Grove, IL: IVP Academic, 2006), 63-86.

[11]In the narrative itself Luke refers especially to the Eleven (1:2), but they become paradigmatic, rather than exclusive, witnesses (see 2:33; 22:14-15, 18; 23:11; 26:16). Luke writes history, but ancient historiography usually deliberately provided role models. For the Twelve as the witnesses, cf. Max Turner, "Every Believer as a Witness in Acts?—in Dialogue with John Michael Penney," *AshTJ* 30 (1998): 57-71; Andreas J. Köstenberger and Peter T. O'Brien, *Salvation to the Ends of the Earth: A Biblical Theology of Mission* (Downers Grove: InterVarsity, 2001), 126-27; but even the immediate context indicated witnesses present for the events beyond the Twelve (Luke 24:33, "those with them"; see Richard J. Dillon, *From Eye-Witnesses to Ministers of the Word* [AnBib 82; Rome: Biblical Institute, 1978], 291). For their paradigmatic role, cf. Roland Gebauer, "Mission und Zeugnis. Zum Verhältnis von missionarischer Wirksamkeit und Zeugenschaft in der Apostelgeschichte," *NovT* 40, no. 1 (1998): 54-72; Peter G. Bolt, "Mission and Witness," 191-214 in *Witness to the Gospel: The Theology of Acts* (ed. I. Howard Marshall and David Peterson; Grand Rapids: Eerdmans, 1998).

[12]On Isaiah in Acts, including Acts 1:8, see especially and most usefully David W. Pao, *Acts and the Isaianic New Exodus* (Grand Rapids: Baker, 2002).

is quoted in Acts 13:47.[13]   In that passage, it applies to Paul's mission,[14] indicating that the mission in Acts applies to the Twelve as well as Jesus's movement of whom they were the most visible representatives and leaders. That is clear because Luke is explicit that the empowerment of the Spirit necessary for the task is not only for the Twelve, but also for all believers (2:38-39), whatever our various roles.

Because ancient writers sometimes stated a thesis or offered a preview toward the beginning of their work,[15] many scholars observe that Acts 1:8 provides a rough outline for all of Acts, which moves from Jerusalem (1-7) to Judea and Samaria (8; 9:31-43) and toward the ends of the earth (10-28).[16] Whereas Luke's Gospel begins and ends with the temple in Jerusalem, Acts moves from Jerusalem to Rome. The overall narrative movement in Acts, then, is from heritage to mission.[17]

So where does Luke envision as being the "ends of the earth?" His contemporaries in the Mediterranean world spoke of the West as Spain and beyond it the "river" (i.e., the ocean).[18] To the East, they thought

---

[13]The exact phrase is quite rare in pre-Lukan Greek literature; see Robert C. Tannehill, *The Acts of the Apostles* (vol. 2 of *The Narrative Unity of Luke-Acts: A Literary Interpretation*; 2 vols.; Minneapolis: Fortress, 1990), 17; followed also by Pao, *Isaianic Exodus*, 94. Most recognize the Isa 49:6 allusion based on Acts 13:47; see e.g., Tannehill, *Acts*, 17; Jacques Dupont, *The Salvation of the Gentiles: Essays on the Acts of the Apostles* (trans. John R. Keating; New York: Paulist, 1979), 18; French L. Arrington, *The Acts of the Apostles: An Introduction and Commentary* (Peabody: Hendrickson, 1988), 9; Thomas S. Moore, "'To the End of the Earth': The Geographical and Ethnic Universalism of Acts 1:8 in Light of Isaianic Influence on Luke," *JETS* 40, no. 3 (1997): 389-99; Pao, *Isaianic Exodus*, 92.

[14]Paul's own letters suggest that he read his own mission in light of them; cf. J. Ross Wagner, *Heralds of the Good News: Isaiah and Paul "In Concert" in the Letter to the Romans* (Leiden: Brill, 2002), 32-33 (more fully, see 29-33).

[15]Cf. e.g., Thucydides 1.23.6; Pliny *N.H.* 8.1.1; 18.1.1; 33.1.1; 34.1.1; 36.1.1; 37.1.1; Philostratus *Vit. Apoll.* 7.1; 8.1.

[16]E.g., Tannehill, *Acts*, 9; Ben Witherington III, *The Acts of the Apostles: A Socio-Rhetorical Commentary* (Grand Rapids: Eerdmans, 1998), 106; Martin Hengel, "The Geography of Palestine in Acts," 27-78 in *The Book of Acts in Its Palestinian Setting* (ed. Richard Bauckham; vol. 4 in The Book of Acts in Its First Century Setting; Grand Rapids: Eerdmans; Carlisle: Paternoster, 1995), 35; Marguerat, *Actes*, 20.

[17]A central argument in my Acts commentary, [*Acts: An Exegetical Commentary*, 4 vols (Grand Rapids, MI: Baker Academic, 2015)], but often emphasized, though stated differently, especially as "from Jerusalem to Rome" (e.g., Homer A. Kent, *Jerusalem to Rome: Studies in the Book of Acts* [Grand Rapids: Baker, 1972]).

[18]For Spain, see e.g., Strabo 1.1.5, 8; 3.2; Seneca *Nat. Q.* 1.pref.13; Silius Italicus 1.270; 15.638; Pliny *Ep.* 2.3.8; *Greek Anthology* 4.3.84-85; for Oceanus, see e.g., Pliny *N.H.* 2.67.167; Philostratus *Hrk.* 8.13.

of such regions as Parthia and beyond it India[19] and China.[20] They knew of peoples to the North, such as Scythians, Germans, and Britons and of a place called Thule (possibly Iceland).[21] They thought of the South as what they called "Ethiopia," meaning Africa south of Egypt.[22] In addition to important trade ties with China over the Silk Road and Roman merchants traveling as far as Vietnam,[23] the Mediterranean world had trade ties as far south in Africa as Tanzania.[24] The most common sense of "Ethiopia" involved the Nubian kingdom of Meroë, so that Philip was already proleptically reaching the southern ends of the earth when he shared the good news with an official from that kingdom later (8:26-40).[25]

Thus, the ends of the earth does not simply mean Rome, where Luke's narrative ends.[26] Rome is, however, strategic, because Luke

---

[19]Contrasting Spain and India as opposite ends of the earth, see Strabo 1.1.8; Seneca *Nat. Q.* 1.pref.13; Juvenal *Sat.* 10.1-2.

[20]China was well known, and the Roman empire had trade ties there; e.g., Pliny *N.H.* 12.1.2; 12.41.84; Lionel Casson, *The Ancient Mariners: Seafarers and Sea Fighters of the Mediterranean in Ancient Times* (2nd ed.; Princeton, NJ: Princeton University Press,1991), 198, 206. China also knew of Rome (Lin Ying, "Ruler of the Treasure Country: The Image of the Roman Empire in Chinese Society from the First to the Fourth Century AD," *Latomus* 63, no. 2 [2004]: 327-39), and the "Silk Road" already functioned by this period (Kevin Herbert, "The Silk Road: The Link between the Classical World and Ancient China," *Classical Bulletin* 73, no. 2 [1997]: 119-24).

[21]On Thule at the ends of the earth, see e.g., Seneca *Med.* 379; Pliny *N.H.* 4.16.104; Eric Herbert Warmington and Martin J. Millett, "Thule," 1521-22 in *OCD*.

[22]E.g., Strabo 1.1.6; Paus. 1.33.3-6; Josephus *Ant.* 11.33, 186, 216, 272; see further Clarice J. Martin, "A Chamberlain's Journey and the Challenge of Interpretation for Liberation," *Semeia* 47 (1989): 105-35, here 118-19; T. C. G. Thornton, "To the end of the earth: Acts 1:8," *ExpT* 89, no. 12 (1978): 374-75; James M. Scott, "Luke's Geographical Horizon," 483-544 in *The Book of Acts in Its Graeco-Roman Setting* (ed. David W. J. Gill and Conrad Gempf; vol. 2 in The Book of Acts in Its First Century Setting; 6 vols.; Grand Rapids: Eerdmans; Carlisle: Paternoster, 1994), 536; Martin Hengel, *Acts and the History of Earliest Christianity* (trans. John Bowden; London: SCM, 1979; Philadelphia: Fortress, 1980), 80; Witherington, *Acts*, 290.

[23]Casson, *Mariners*, 205 (also noting trade "with Malaya and Java").

[24]J. Nelson Kraybill, *Imperial Cult and Commerce in John's Apocalypse* (JSNTSup 132; Sheffield: Sheffield Academic Press, 1996), 104.

[25]It proleptically foreshadows the future mission to the south (Martin, "Chamberlain's Journey"; Craig Keener, "The Aftermath of the Ethiopian Eunuch," *A.M.E. Church Review* 118, no. 385 [Jan. 2003]: 112-24). Favoring the historical plausibility of that narrative, see Craig Keener, "Novels' 'Exotic' Places and Luke's African Official (Acts 8:27)," *AUSS* 46, no. 1 (2008): 5-20.

[26]Cf. also Tannehill, *Acts*, 17; Jacob Jervell, *Die Apostelgeschichte* (KEKNT 17; Göttingen: Vandenhoeck & Ruprecht, 1998), 116; Beverly Roberts Gaventa, *The Acts of the Apostles* (ANTC; Nashville: Abingdon, 2003), 65-66; Bertram Melbourne, "Acts 1:8: Where on Earth Is the End of the Earth?" 1-14 in *2000 Years of Christianity in Africa* (ed. Emory J. Tolbert; n.p.: Sabbath in Africa Study Group, 2005), esp. 11-14.

writes to people in the Roman Empire, for whom the evangelization of Rome would impact their sphere. Paul reaching Rome in Acts 28 is a proleptic fulfillment of the mission, like Philip preaching to the African official or Peter preaching to the diaspora crowds present at the feast of Pentecost. Acts does not conclude with the completion of the mission, but rather offers a model for its continuance to "the ends of the earth," including parts of the world that Luke's audience could not have known about.[27]

We may add that, if any starting point was privileged, it was Jerusalem (cf. also Rom 15:19), but otherwise God's people have just started where they were.[28] When the West sent most missionaries, the West may have been their own practical starting point, but missions has never been a distinctly western idea. Indeed, in ancient Mediterranean conceptualizations of the world, the movement of the gospel from Jerusalem to Rome specifically involved an Asian movement that missionized southern Europe.[29]

Another biblical allusion appears in 1:9-11, in addition to that in 1:8. This one, like the allusion to Isaiah noted above, also implies Spirit-empowered witness, because it evokes the model of prophetic empowerment. In 1:9-11, Jesus ascends to heaven after promising the Spirit. The most obvious allusion to an ascension that Luke could expect all of his biblically informed audience to catch is an allusion to

---

[27]On the open-endedness of Acts, see e.g., James D. G. Dunn, *The Acts of the Apostles* (Valley Forge, PA: Trinity Press International, 1996), 278; Daniel Marguerat, *La Première Histoire du Christianisme (Les Actes des apôtres)* (LD 180; Paris, Genève: Les Éditions du Cerf, 1999), 333; idem, *The First Christian Historian: Writing the 'Acts of the Apostles'* (SNTSMS 121; trans. Ken McKinney, Gregory J. Laughery and Richard Bauckham; Cambridge: Cambridge University Press, 2002), 152-54, 230; Brian Rosner, "The Progress of the Word," 215-34 in *Witness to the Gospel*, 232-33. Open or incomplete endings were frequent in ancient literature (e.g., Dionysius of Halicarnassus *Demosth.* 58; Valerius Maximus 9.15. ext. 2; Plutarch *Fame Ath.* 8, *Mor.* 351B; *Fort. Alex.* 2.13, *Mor.* 345B; *Fort. Rom.* 13, *Mor.* 326C; *Uned. R.* 7, *Mor.* 782F; Isocrates *Demon.* 52, *Or.* 1; Demetrius *Style* 5.304; Hdn 8.8.8; *L.A.B.*; Mk 16:8; especially J. Lee Magness, *Sense and Absence: Structure and Suspension in the Ending of Mark's Gospel* [SBLSemS; Atlanta: Society of Biblical Literature, 1986]).

[28]For such local applications, see e.g., Musimbi Kanyoro, "Thinking Mission in Africa," 61-70 in *The Feminist Companion to the Acts of the Apostles* (ed. Amy-Jill Levine with Marianne Blickenstaff; Cleveland, OH: Pilgrim; Edinburgh: T & T Clark International, 2004), 62. On Jerusalem's theological, salvation-historical priority, see e.g., Dunn, *Acts*, 3-4.

[29]See Craig Keener, "Between Asia and Europe: Postcolonial Mission in Acts 16:8-10," *AJPS* 11 (January/July 2008).

Elijah.[30] When Elijah ascended to heaven, he left for his successor, Elisha, the double portion of the Spirit that had rested on him (2 Kings 2:9-14).[31] As that Old Testament account provided for the transition between narratives about Elijah's ministry and those about Elisha's, so the present account functions as a transition between Jesus's ministry in Luke's Gospel and that of his appointed agents in Acts.[32] Again, we see an allusion to the same Spirit who empowered the prophets.

The Preparation for Pentecost (1:12-26)

Although the preparation for Pentecost will be addressed much more briefly than the promise of Pentecost, this account is, nonetheless, also crucial to Luke's point. Part of the narrative involves re-establishing the leadership structure of the Twelve, presumably (as in some other ancient models) as an expression of the expectation in Israel's restoration.[33] For them to restore the leadership structure was to prepare for Jesus's promise in faith. Although salvation-historical events happen only when God is ready, he allows those who trust him

---

[30]On Gentile ascension narratives more generally, see e.g., Charles H. Talbert, "The Myth of a Descending-Ascending Redeemer in Mediterranean Antiquity," *NTS* 22, no. 4 (July 1976): 418-40; Rick Strelan, *Strange Acts: Studies in the Cultural World of the Acts of the Apostles* (BZNW 126; Berlin, New York: Walter de Gruyter, 2004), 42-47; Wilfried Eckey, *Die Apostelgeschichte: Der Weg des Evangeliums von Jerusalem nach Rom* (2 vols.; Neukirchen-Vluyn: Neukirchener Verlag, 2000), 57-60; for the closer Jewish ascension narratives, see e.g., Arie W. Zwiep, *The Ascension of the Messiah in Lukan Christology* (NovTSup 87; Leiden: Brill, 1997), 41-75; Paul Palatty, "The Ascension of Christ in Lk-Acts (An exegetical critical study of Lk 24,50-53 and Acts 1,2-3, 9-11)," *Bible Bhashyam* 12, no. 2 (1986): 100-17.

[31]For this biblical account as the closest model, see also e.g., Zwiep, *Ascension*, 59-63, 194; Kenneth Duncan Litwak, *Echoes of Scripture in Luke-Acts: Telling the History of God's People Intertextually* (JSNTSup 282; London, New York: T&T Clark International, 2005), 149-50.

[32]On succession narratives and Acts, see Charles H. Talbert, *Reading Luke-Acts in its Mediterranean Milieu* (NovTSup 107; Leiden: Brill, 2003), 19-55 (though most scholars do not find as much biographic character in Acts as Talbert does).

[33]See discussion in Turner, *Power*, 301; Pao, *Isaianic Exodus*, 123-29. Most scholars recognize the choice of the Twelve as symbolizing a restoration movement, analogous to 1QS 8.1-2; 4Q259 2.9 (Joachim Jeremias, *New Testament Theology* [New York: Charles Scribner's Sons, 1971], 234-35; F. F. Bruce, "Jesus and the Gospels in the Light of the Scrolls," 70-82 in *The Scrolls and Christianity: Historical and Theological Significance* [ed. Matthew Black; London: S.P.C.K., 1969], 75-76; James H. Charlesworth, *Jesus within Judaism: New Light from Exciting Archaeological Discoveries* [ABRL; New York: Doubleday, 1988], 138; E. P. Sanders, *Jesus and Judaism* [Philadelphia: Fortress, 1985], 104).

to prepare for those happenings in advance (e.g., 1 Chron 22:14-16; 28:11-19; Amos 3:7).

A key element that frames the section about preparing for the Spirit's coming is the emphasis on prayer together and unity (Acts 1:14; 2:1). Prayer is a frequent theme in Luke-Acts,[34] and often precedes the coming of the Spirit there.[35] Thus, of the four Gospels, only Luke mentions that the Spirit descended on Jesus as he was praying (Luke 3:21-22). When the assembly of believers prayed together in Acts 4:31, they were filled with the Spirit; Peter and John prayed for the Samaritans to receive the Spirit (8:15); Saul was filled with the Spirit (9:17) after he had been praying (9:11); and the Spirit likewise fell on Cornelius and his guests (10:44), and Cornelius had been praying (10:30).

Although Luke does not always associate the Spirit with prayer, the connection is frequent enough, and sometimes clear enough (especially in 4:31), to reinforce the importance of prayer in preparing for the Spirit's coming. Luke's first volume is most explicit on this point, the discussion of prayer in Luke 11:1-13 climaxing in prayer's chief object—i.e., the gift of God's own person and presence, namely,

---

[34]See e.g., François Bovon, *Luke the Theologian: Thirty-Three Years of Research (1950-1983)* (trans. Ken McKinney; Allison Park, PA: Pickwick Publications, 1987), 400-3; Allison A. Trites, "The Prayer Motif in Luke-Acts," 168-86 in *Perspectives on Luke-Acts* (ed. Charles H. Talbert; Danville, VA: Association of Baptist Professors of Religion; Edinburgh: T. & T. Clark, 1978); Robert J. Karris, *What Are They Saying about Luke and Acts? A Theology of the Faithful God* (New York: Paulist, 1979), 74-83; Steven F. Plymale, *The Prayer Texts of Luke-Acts* (AUSt 7, Theology and Religion 118; New York: Peter Lang, 1991); Kyu Sam Han, "Theology of Prayer in the Gospel of Luke," *JETS* 43, no. 4 (2000): 675-93; Ignatius Jesudasan, "Prayer in the Acts of the Apostles," *Journal of Dharma* 28, no. 4 (2003): 543-48; Michael Green, *Thirty Years that Changed the World: The Book of Acts for Today* (Grand Rapids, Cambridge: Eerdmans, 2002), 268-73; Frank Thielman, *Theology of the New Testament* (Grand Rapids: Zondervan, 2005), 142-46; David Crump, *Jesus the Intercessor: Prayer and Christology in Luke-Acts* (Grand Rapids: Baker, 1999; originally WUNT 2.49; Tübingen: Mohr-Siebeck, 1992); S. John Roth, "Jesus the Pray-er," *CurTM* 33, no. 6 (Dec. 2006): 488-500; Peter T. O'Brien, "Prayer in Luke-Acts," *TynBul* 24 (1973): 111-27.

[35]For the connection, cf. e.g., J. H. E. Hull, *The Holy Spirit in the Acts of the Apostles* (London: Lutterworth, 1967; Cleveland: The World Publishing Company, 1968), 48; Earl Richard, "Pentecost as a Recurrent Theme in Luke-Acts," 133-49 in *New Views on Luke and Acts* (ed. Earl Richard; Collegeville, MN: Glazier, Liturgical Press, 1990), 135; Ju Hur, *A Dynamic Reading of the Holy Spirit in Luke-Acts* (JSNTSup 211; Sheffield: Sheffield Academic Press, 2001), 270. The point need not be prayer for the Spirit so much as the Spirit coming to prayerful people (Graham H. Twelftree, "Prayer and the Coming of the Spirit in Acts," *ExpT* 117, no. 7 [2006]: 271-76).

the Holy Spirit. In that passage, Jesus promises that God will not withhold this blessing from any who ask and seek insistently for it.[36]

The Proofs of Pentecost (2:2-4)

Three signs publicly demonstrate the Spirit's coming on the day of Pentecost—wind (2:2), fire (2:3), and worship in languages unknown to the speakers (2:4).[37] Of the three, the third calls for the greatest comment.

The wind and fire here both evoke earlier biblical theophanies (e.g., Exod 3:2; 2 Sam 5:24; 1 Kings 19:11-12; Job 38:1; Ps 29:3-10; 97:2-5; 104:3; Isa 6:4; 29:6; 30:27-28; 66:15; Ezek 1:4),[38] and scholars often compare them with phenomena accompanying God's revelation at Sinai (Exod 19:16-20; Deut 4:11, 24).[39] Moreover, these theophanic elements recall a theme observed earlier—the Spirit coming as a foretaste (initial experience) of the future world.[40] Wind evokes the image of end-time resurrection life that may be inferred in Ezekiel 37:9,

---

[36]The context may involve persistence, but it probably also involves the issue of honor and shame, perhaps the honor of God bound up with his promise or with the need of his people (see Kenneth Ewing Bailey, *Poet and Peasant: A Literary Cultural Approach to the Parables in Luke* [Grand Rapids: Eerdmans, 1976], 126-28; Alan F. Johnson, "Assurance for Man: The Fallacy of Translating *Anaideia* by 'Persistence' in Luke 11:5-8," *JETS* 22, no. 2 [June 1979]: 125-31; E. W. Huffard, "The Parable of the Friend at Midnight: God's Honor or Man's Persistence?" *Restoration Quarterly* 21, no. 3 [1978]: 154-60).

[37]I treated Acts 2 at greater length in Keener, *Spirit*, 190-213; and especially in my Acts: An Exegetical Commentary, vol. 1.

[38]Cf. also *Jub.* 1:3; *L.A.E.* 25:3; *4 Ezra* 3:19; for Greek analogies to theophanies, cf. Pieter W. Van der Horst, "Hellenistic Parallels to the Acts of the Apostles," *JSNT* 25 (Oct. 1985): 49-60, here 49-50. In the context of Elijah's succession, see 2 Kings 2:11.

[39]E.g., Jervell, *Apostelgeschichte*, 133, 138; Matthias Wenk, *Community-Forming Power: The Socio-Ethical Role of the Spirit in Luke-Acts* (JPTSup 19; Sheffield: Sheffield Academic Press, 2000), 246-51; Joseph A. Fitzmyer, *The Acts of the Apostles: A New Translation with Introduction and Commentary* (AB 31; New York: Doubleday, 1998), 234. Scholars differ on whether this passage in Acts contains specific allusions to Sinai, however.

[40]Cf. also e.g., C. F. Sleeper, "Pentecost and Resurrection," *JBL* 84 (Dec. 1965): 389-99, here 390; William Barclay, "Acts ii.14-40," *ExpT* 70 (1958-59): 196-99, here 198-99; Henry J. Cadbury, "Acts and Eschatology," 300-11 in *The Background of the New Testament and Its Eschatology: Essays in honour of Charles Harold Dodd* (ed. W. D. Davies and D. Daube; Cambridge: Cambridge University, 1964), 300; A. P. O'Hagan, "The First Christian Pentecost (Acts 2:1-13)," *SBFLA* 23 (1973): 50-66; M.-É. Boismard and A. Lamouille, *Les Actes des Deux Apôtres* (Études Bibliques, n.s. 12; 3 vols.; Paris: Librairie Lecoffre, 1990), 2:101.

14;[41] whereas fire often evokes eschatological judgment,[42] including when paired with the Spirit in Luke 3:9, 16-17.[43] The eschatological era was breaking into the present, a point reinforced explicitly by Peter's opening explanation that the outpoured prophetic Spirit demonstrated the arrival of the "last days," the eschatological time of salvation (2:17, 20-21).

Tongues, however, is the most significant of the three signs for Luke, it being repeated at subsequent outpourings in 10:46 and 19:6. This speaking in tongues is also more strategic for Luke's narrative because what follows hinges on it—that tongues provides the catalyst for the multi-cultural audience's recognition of God's activity (2:5-13) and the starting point for Peter's message, "This is what Joel meant . . . " (2:16-17).

Further, tongues does not appear here arbitrarily as one possible sign among many. Instead, it relates to Acts' central theme articulated in 1:8—i.e., Spirit-inspired, cross-cultural witness. Luke recounts that those in the Upper Room were "speaking in other languages even as the Spirit was giving them inspired utterance" (2:4). Peter goes on to explain the phenomenon biblically as a form of inspired, prophetic speech, noting that it fulfills Joel's prediction that God's people would prophesy (2:17-18).

But Luke's emphasis in 1:8 is prophetic witness for Christ, bringing the "word of the Lord" (e.g., 8:25; 12:24; 13:48-49). Why then does he choose to point to tongues as an important example of this, mentioning it at three distinct outpourings of the Spirit? Undoubtedly, he

---

[41]For this background here, see e.g., Joseph A. Grassi, "Ezekiel xxxvii.1-14 and the New Testament," *NTS* 11, no. 2 (Jan. 1965): 162-64, here 164; F. F. Bruce, *Commentary on the Book of the Acts: The English Text with Introduction, Exposition and Notes* (NICNT; Grand Rapids: Eerdmans, 1977), 54; Richard N. Longenecker, *Acts* (ExpBC; Grand Rapids: Zondervan, 1995), 66; Eddie Gibbs, "The Launching of Mission: The Outpouring of the Spirit at Pentecost, Acts 2:1-41," 18-28 in *Mission in Acts: Ancient Narratives in Contemporary Context* (ed. Robert L. Gallagher and Paul Hertig; AmSocMissS 34; Maryknoll, NY: Orbis, 2004), 21.

[42]E.g., Isa 26:11; 66:15-16, 24; CD 2.4-6; *1 En.* 103:8; *Sib. Or.* 4.43, 161, 176-78; 2 Thess 1:6-7.

[43]See discussion in Menzies, *Development*, 137-44; Keener, *Spirit*, 127. Cf. also Luke 12:49-50 (as understood in John A. T. Robinson, *Twelve New Testament Studies* [SBT 34; London: SCM, 1962], 161; James D. G. Dunn, *Baptism in the Holy Spirit: A Re-examination of the New Testament Teaching on the Gift of the Spirit in relation to Pentecostalism Today* [SBT, 2d ser., 15; London: SCM, 1970], 42).

emphasizes the connection between tongues and the Spirit because it so well symbolizes his theme of Spirit-empowered cross-cultural witness. If God's people can worship him in other people's languages, how much more can they share the good news through languages that they share in common? In other words, worshiping God in other people's languages shows that he has empowered the Church to cross all cultural and linguistic barriers with his gospel.[44]

Here is where the early Pentecostals picked up on a connection that most (though not all) traditional scholars historically missed.[45] Late nineteenth-century radical evangelicals stressed holiness, missions, and healing. Many sought what they called the "baptism in the Holy Spirit" and were praying for God to provide "missionary tongues," which they believed were supernaturally endowed languages that would enable them to skip the lengthy process of language-learning in missions.[46]

---

[44]See Craig S. Keener, "Why Does Luke Use Tongues as a Sign of the Spirit's Empowerment?" *JPT* 15, no. 2 (2007): 177-84; idem, *3 Crucial Questions about the Holy Spirit* (Grand Rapids: Baker, 1996), 69; idem, *Gift & Giver: The Holy Spirit for Today* (Grand Rapids: Baker, 2001), 180; John V. York, *Missions in the Age of the Spirit* (foreword by Byron D. Klaus; Springfield, MO: Logion, 2000), 80, 185-86; Francis Watson, *Paul, Judaism, and the Gentiles: Beyond the New Perspective* (rev. ed.; Grand Rapids: Eerdmans, 2007), 68-69; cf. earlier e.g., William Wrede, *The Messianic Secret* (trans. J. C. G. Greig; reprint, Cambridge: James Clarke & Company, 1971), 232; Alfred Wikenhauser, *Die Apostelgeschichte übersetzt und erklärt* (RNT 5; Regensburg: Pustet, 1938; 4th ed., 1961), 38; R. P. C. Hanson, *The Acts in the Revised Standard Version, With Introduction and Commentary* (Oxford: Clarendon, 1967), 63-64; and especially George Eldon Ladd, *The Young Church* (New York: Abingdon, 1964), 56; Dupont, *Salvation*, 52, 59; Krister Stendahl, *Paul Among Jews and Gentiles and Other Essays* (Philadelphia: Fortress, 1976), 118-19; John J. Kilgallen, *A Brief Commentary on the Acts of the Apostles* (New York, Mahwah: Paulist, 1988), 16.

[45]Still, some others have seen the connection between tongues and crosscultural ministry or unity, especially earlier in history; see e.g., Origen *Comm. Rom.* on Rom 1:14; Chrysostom *Hom. Cor.* 35.1; Bede *Comm. Acts* 2.3A; Leo the Great *Sermon* 75.2; more recently, cf. J. W. Packer, *Acts of the Apostles* (Cambridge Bible Commentary; Cambridge: University Press, 1966), 27; and most scholars listed above.

[46]See e.g., Allan Anderson, *An Introduction to Pentecostalism: Global Charismatic Christianity* (Cambridge: Cambridge University, 2004), 33-34; Gary B. McGee, "The Radical Strategy in Modern Mission: The Linkage of Paranormal Phenomena with Evangelism," 69-95 in *The Holy Spirit and Mission Dynamics* (ed. C. Douglas McConnell; Evangelical Missiological Society Series 5; Pasadena: William Carey, 1997), 77-78, 80-83.

These early Pentecostals sought both missionary tongues and the Spirit for empowerment for mission.[47]   Many who then left for foreign countries to try out their missionary tongues were cruelly disappointed. Although Pentecostals kept tongues for prayer (1 Cor 14:13-14), most abandoned the missionary-tongues idea.[48]   Yet at the risk of sounding controversial, I believe they were right about the connection between missions and tongues-speaking that they saw in Acts. Granted, neither in Acts nor in early Pentecostalism did tongues provide a substitute for language-learning. (Nor, I might add regretfully, does it usually perform that service for scholars preparing for their doctoral language exams.) While people have   sometimes

---

[47]Gary B. McGee, "Early Pentecostal Hermeneutics: Tongues as Evidence in the Book of Acts," 96-118 in *Initial Evidence: Historical and Biblical Perspectives on the Pentecostal Doctrine of Spirit Baptism* (ed. Gary B. McGee; Peabody: Hendrickson, 1991), 102; idem, "The Radical Strategy," 47-59 in *Signs & Wonders in Ministry Today* (ed. Benny C. Aker and Gary B. McGee; foreword by Thomas E. Trask; Springfield, MO: Gospel Publishing House, 1996), 52-53; James R. Goff. Jr., "Initial Tongues in the Theology of Charles Fox Parham," 57-71 in *Initial Evidence: Historical and Biblical Perspectives on the Pentecostal Doctrine of Spirit Baptism* (ed. Gary B. McGee; Peabody: Hendrickson, 1991), 64-65; Douglas Jacobsen, *Thinking in the Spirit: Theologies of the Early Pentecostal Movement* (Bloomington, IN: Indiana University, 2003), 25, 49-50, 74, 76, 97; Cecil M. Robeck, Jr., *The Azusa Street Mission & Revival: The Birth of the Global Pentecostal Movement* (Nashville: Thomas Nelson, 2006), 41-42, 236-37, 243, 252; see especially Gary B. McGee, "Shortcut to Language Preparation? Radical Evangelicals, Missions, and the Gift of Tongues," *IBMR* 25 (July 2001): 118-23.

[48]Grant Wacker, *Heaven Below: Early Pentecostals and American Culture* (Cambridge: Harvard University, 2001), 47-51; Gary B. McGee, *People of the Spirit: The Assemblies of God* (Springfield, MO: Gospel Publishing House, 2004), 77-78; Neil Hudson, "Strange Words and Their Impact on Early Pentecostals: A Historical Perspective," 52-80 in *Speaking in Tongues: Multi-Disciplinary Perspectives* (ed. Mark J. Cartledge; SPCI; Waynesboro, GA; Bletchley, Milton Keynes, UK: Paternoster, 2006), 61-63; Allan Anderson, "To All Points of the Compass: The Azusa Street Revival and Global Pentecostalism," *Enrichment* 11, no. 2 (2006): 164-72, here 167; especially Gary B. McGee, "Strategies for Global Mission," 203-24 in *Called & Empowered: Global Mission in Pentecostal Perspective* (ed. Murray A. Dempster, Byron D. Klaus and Douglas Petersen; Peabody, MA: Hendrickson, 1991), 204 (noting its waning already by 1906). By contrast, Parham never abandoned it (Anderson, *Pentecostalism*, 190).

recognized the languages spoken,[49] that does not seem to be the primary purpose of the gift.

Yet tongues is important precisely because it aptly illustrates Luke's emphasis on the power of the Spirit to speak for God across cultural barriers. Tongues is not an arbitrary sign, but a sign that God has empowered his servants to exalt him in others' languages. Even among charismatic scholars, there is not absolute agreement whether every individual who receives this empowerment prays in tongues.[50] Nevertheless, those who observe Luke's narrative closely should recognize (whatever their own experience or theology) that tongues evidences the character of the experience that God has empowered his witnesses to cross-cultural barriers with his gospel.

It is probably no coincidence that Pentecostalism within just one century experienced perhaps the most massive growth rates of any Christian movement in history, given that it was birthed in a context that emphasized holiness (i.e., uncompromised devotion to God), prayer, faith, and missions. Of course, that connection also serves as a warning, because many movements that began with such emphases and growth rates eventually cooled and were supplanted by other movements of God's Spirit.

We do not retain the Spirit merely by retaining a heritage or tradition that enshrines a past experience of the Spirit or by simply repeating what our predecessors have done. As we have seen, the earliest Pentecostals were flexible, correcting their ideas where

---

[49]E.g., Wayne E. Warner, *The Woman Evangelist: The Life and Times of Charismatic Evangelist Maria B. Woodworth-Etter* (Studies in Evangelicalism 8; Metuchen, NJ: Scarecrow, 1986), 256-57; Rex Gardner, *Healing Miracles: A doctor investigates* (London: Darton, Longman and Todd, 1986), 38, 142-43; McGee, "Shortcut"; idem, *People of Spirit*, 24, 46-47, 57, 61, 64, 75; Robeck, *Mission*, 268-69; Gordon Lindsay, *John G. Lake: Apostle to Africa* (Dallas, TX: Christ for the Nations, 1981), 25, 27; Edith Blumhofer, "Portrait of a Generation: Azusa Street Comes to Chicago," *Enrichment* 11, no. 2 (2006): 95-102, here 96, 99; Vinson Synan, *Voices of Pentecost: Testimonies of Lives Touched by the Holy Spirit* (Ann Arbor, MI: Servant Publications, 2003), 60, 76-77, 84, 101-2; most extensively, Ralph W. Harris, *Acts Today: Signs & Wonders of the Holy Spirit* (Springfield, MO: Gospel Publishing House, 1995), 108-30; Jordan Daniel May, *Global Witnesses to Pentecost: The Testimony of "Other Tongues"* (Cleveland, TN: CPT Press, 2013).

[50]See e.g., Henry I. Lederle, "Initial Evidence and the Charismatic Movement: An Ecumenical Appraisal," 131-41 in *Initial Evidence*; earlier, see e.g., McGee, "Hermeneutics," 107-10; Jacobsen, *Thinking in Spirit*, 293, 314-13, 395 n. 4.

needed.[51] To maintain the blessing that inaugurated Pentecostalism, we need what made it really work, which is God's Spirit. As we noted at the very outset, we cannot do his work without him.

The Peoples of Pentecost (2:5-13)

Luke's narrative goes on to reinforce the point just observed with a proleptic foreshadowing of the gospel reaching the ends of the earth. He indicates the presence of diaspora Jews "from every nation under heaven" (2:5). Although they are Jewish, the breadth of their geographic exposure foreshadows the mission to the nations laid out in 1:8,[52] just like the African "ends of the earth" in 8:26-40 or evangelizing in the heart of the Roman Empire in 28:16-31.

Although there is no absolute consensus, most think that Luke here is alluding back to the account of the Tower of Babel.[53] (This was the view of many ancient commentators,[54] early Pentecostals,[55] and

---

[51]Early Pentecostalism exhibited flexibility on secondary theological questions (Henry I. Lederle, *Treasures Old and New: Interpretations of "Spirit-Baptism" in the Charismatic Renewal Movement* [Peabody: Hendrickson, 1988], 29-31, esp. 29; see also Walter J. Hollenweger, *The Pentecostals* [Peabody: Hendrickson, 1988; reprint of London: SCM, 1972], 32, 331-36). Among more recent examples of change: today Pentecostal scholarship is flourishing. The Spirit's shaping of our intellectual perspectives, though not always emphasized traditionally, is important (cf. Craig Keener, "'Fleshly' versus Spirit Perspectives in Romans 8:5-8," 211-29 in *Paul: Jew, Greek and Roman* [ed. Stanley Porter; PAST 5; Leiden: Brill, 2008]).

[52]Cf. e.g., Martin Dibelius, *Studies in the Acts of the Apostles* (ed. H. Greeven. Trans. M. Ling; New York: Charles Scribner's Sons, 1956), 106; F. J. Foakes-Jackson, *The Acts of the Apostles* (MNTC; London: Hodder & Stoughton, 1931), 11; Robinson, *Studies*, 167.

[53]E.g., C. F. D. Moule, *Christ's Messengers: Studies in the Acts of the Apostles* (New York: Association, 1957), 23; Bruce, *Commentary*, 64; Justo L. González, *Acts: The Gospel of the Spirit* (Maryknoll, NY: Orbis, 2001), 39; Stendahl, *Paul*, 117; Bert B. Dominy, "Spirit, Church, and Mission: Theological Implications of Pentecost," *SWJT* 35, no. 2 (1993): 34-39; D. Smith, "What Hope After Babel? Diversity and Community in Gen 11:1-9; Exod 1:1-14; Zeph 3:1-13 and Acts 2:1-13," *HBC* 18, no. 2 (1996): 169-91; F. Scott Spencer, *Acts* (Sheffield: Sheffield Academic Press, 1997), 32-33; Georgette Chéreau, "De Babel à la Pentecôte. Histoire d'une bénédiction," *NRTh* 122, no. 1 (2000): 19-36; Alexander Venter, *Doing Reconciliation: Racism, Reconciliation and Transformation in the Church and World* (Cape Town, South Africa: Vineyard International Publishing, 2004), 155; Max Turner, "Early Christian Experience and Theology of 'Tongues'—A New Testament Perspective," 1-33 in *Speaking in Tongues: Multi-Disciplinary Perspectives* (ed. Mark J. Cartledge; SPCI; Waynesboro, GA; Bletchley, Milton Keynes, UK: Paternoster, 2006), 32.

[54]Cyril of Jerusalem *Catechetical Lecture* 17.16-17; Arator *Acts* 1; Bede *Comm. Acts* 2.4; patristic sources in Marguerat, *Actes*, 81 n. 45.

[55]Anderson, *Pentecostalism*, 44.

now modern scholars.) Luke provides a list of nations from which these Jewish worshipers come (2:9-11), a list that would evoke most easily the Bible's first listing of nations in Genesis 10.[56] That list was followed in the next chapter by God coming down to "scatter the languages."[57] Whereas he did so then in judgment, he does so here to bring a new cross-cultural unity in the Spirit.[58]

Cross-cultural unity is a major activity of the Spirit. The Azusa Street Revival occurred in a historical context of revivals elsewhere in the world, including the Welsh Revival and the outpouring of the Spirit at Pandita Ramabai's orphanage in India. The major human figure providing leadership in the Azusa Street Revival was William Seymour, an African-American man of prayer, at a time of severe racial segregation in the United States.   Azusa Street was indeed multi-cultural.[59] One of its participants, Frank Bartleman, a white American, celebrated that "The color line was washed away by the blood."[60]

---

[56]E.g., Scott, "Horizon," 529-30. The geographic content is similar (Goulder, *Type and History*, 153-54, 158; Moule, *Messengers*, 24); early Judaism continued to use this list of nations, as noted in Scott, "Horizon," 507-22; idem, "Geographical Perspectives in Late Antiquity," 411-14 in *Dictionary of New Testament Background* (ed. Craig A. Evans and Stanley E. Porter; Downers Grove, IL: InterVarsity, 2000), 412-13; idem, *Paul and the Nations: The Old Testament and Jewish Background of Paul's Mission to the Nations with Special Reference to the Destination of Galatians* (WUNT 84; Tübingen: Mohr [Siebeck], 1995); Dean Philip Bechard, *Paul Outside the Walls: A Study of Luke's Socio-Geographical Universalism in Acts 14:8-20* (AnBib 143; Rome: Editrice Pontificio Istituto Biblico, 2000), 209-31.

[57]With Goulder, *Type and History*, 158.

[58]Cf. González, *Acts*, 39; Hinne Wagenaar, "Babel, Jerusalem and Kumba: Missiological Reflections on Genesis 11:1-9 and Acts 2:1-13," *IntRevMiss* 92, no. 366 (2003): 406-21; Frank D. Macchia, "Babel and the Tongues of Pentecost: Reversal or Fulfilment? A Theological Perspective," 34-51 in *Speaking in Tongues: Multi-Disciplinary Perspectives* (ed. Mark J. Cartledge; SPCI; Waynesboro, GA; Bletchley, Milton Keynes, UK: Paternoster Press, 2006).

[59]See Robeck, *Mission*, 88, 137-38; testimony in Stanley M. Horton, *I & II Corinthians: A Logion Press Commentary* (Springfield, MO: Logion, Gospel Publishing House, 1999), 66 n. 29; cf. Vinson Synan, *The Holiness-Pentecostal Movement in the United States* (Grand Rapids: Eerdmans, 1971), 80, 109-11, 165-69, 172, 178-79, 182-83, 221; idem, "Seymour, William Joseph," 778-81 in *Dictionary of Pentecostal and Charismatic Movements* (ed. Stanley M. Burgess, Gary B. McGee, and Patrick H. Alexander; Grand Rapids: Zondervan, 1988), 778-81; idem, "The Lasting Legacies of the Azusa Street Revival," *Enrichment* 11, no. 2 (2006): 142-52, here 148-49; Leonard Lovett, "Black Holiness-Pentecostalism." 76-84 in *Dictionary of Pentecostal and Charismatic Movements*, 83; David D. Daniels, III, "God Makes no Differences in Nationality: The Fashioning of a New Racial/Nonracial Identity at the Azusa Street Revival," *Enrichment* 11, no. 2 (2006): 72-76; Jacobsen, *Thinking in Spirit*, 63, 260-62.

[60]Frank Bartleman, *Azusa Street* (foreword by Vinson Synan; Plainfield, NJ: Logos, 1980; reprint of 1925 ed.), 54.

Unfortunately, it was washed away only temporarily before the social realities of Jim Crow laws in the southern U.S. and other factors led to a new segregation.[61] Seymour's white mentor, Charles Parham, criticized the events at Azusa Street in racial terms. Feeling betrayed, Seymour shifted the focus that his preaching emphasized in Acts 2, noting that in Acts 2 the outpouring of the Spirit involved crossing cultural barriers.

The true reception of the Spirit must involve ethnic reconciliation and unity among Christ's followers.[62]   Most nations have minority cultures among them; most of us know of people groups that are despised by or hostile to our own. As Seymour came to emphasize through his bitter experience with Parham, the true experience of the Spirit must go beyond speaking in other people's languages under the inspiration of the Spirit.   We need to work for that unity to which tongues-speaking points.

The remainder of Acts develops this theme. For example, despite the conflict between Hebrews and Hellenists in 6:1, the new Hellenist leaders were themselves full of the Spirit (6:3, 5, 10; 7:51, 55).[63] These bicultural ministers carried the mission forward across a cultural barrier that had not yet been breached by the Twelve, setting the example for them (e.g., 8:25).[64] The Spirit continued to drive God's own resistant people across cultural barriers (8:29; 10:19; 15:28), and God baptized new groups in the Spirit so that they would become the Jerusalem believers' partners in missions, not just recipients of their ministry (8:15-17; 10:44-46; 19:6).

---

[61] Amos Yong, *The Spirit Poured Out on All Flesh: Pentecostalism and the Possibility of Global Theology* (Grand Rapids: Baker, 2005), 72-73; see similarly in India, Yong, *Spirit Poured*, 56-57.

[62] See e.g., Cecil M. Robeck, Jr., "William J. Seymour and 'The Bible Evidence,'" 72-95 in *Initial Evidence*, 81-89; Jacobsen, *Thinking in Spirit*, 78.

[63] The seven selected in 6:5 are surely Hellenists, given that all had Greek names (a unanimity that is surely deliberate, with e.g., Craig C. Hill, *Hellenists and Hebrews: Reappraising Division within the Earliest Church* [Minneapolis: Fortress, 1992], 47). Even in Rome, where only 1% of Jewish inscriptions are in Semitic languages, 15.2% of the names include Semitic elements (Harry J. Leon, *The Jews of Ancient Rome* [Philadelphia: The Jewish Publication Society of America, 1960], 107-8).

[64] For Philip as Peter's "forerunner," in terms of narrative function, see F. Scott Spencer, *The Portrait of Philip in Acts. A Study of Role and Relations* (JSNTSup 67; Sheffield: Sheffield Academic Press, 1992), 220-41.

The Prophecy of Pentecost (2:17-21)

The disciples' worship in other tongues (2:4) fulfilled Joel's prophecy about prophetic empowerment (2:16-18). The gathered crowd, on hearing these praises in many languages (2:6), asks, "What does this mean?" (2:12; cf. 2:11). Peter then responds, "This fulfills what Joel said . . . " about God's people prophesying (2:16-18).[65]

In light of Joel, all God's people are now to be empowered as end-time prophets for Christ. Peter further quotes Joel 2:28-32 but adapts the wording to bring out the meaning (a common Jewish practice).[66] Joel had said that God would pour out the Spirit "afterward"—the context reflecting a period of terrible judgment and the time of Israel's restoration (2:25-27, 3:1). Emphasizing that the eschatological promise was now being fulfilled, Peter adapts the wording in line with the original context, proclaiming that God pours out the Spirit "in the last days" (Acts 2:17). Although "the last days" is eschatological language,[67] this period is being fulfilled already in the present (cf. similarly Rom 8:22; 1 Tim 4:1; 2 Tim 3:1; Heb 1:2; 2 Pet 3:3; Rev 12:5-6, 10). Peter's adaptation underscores the fact that Jesus's first coming had already introduced the end-time, although it will be consummated only with his return.

Peter then adds another line that highlights the prophetic nature of the gift—"And they will prophesy" (2:18). This line simply reiterates what he has already quoted from Joel, that "Your sons and daughters will prophesy." They will also dream dreams and see visions (2:17), which are experiences most typical in biblical history for prophets.

---

[65]For the connection, cf. e.g., Pesch, *Apostelgeschichte*, 1:119.

[66]E.g., Lou H. Silberman, "Unriddling the Riddle: A Study in the Structure and Language of the Habakkuk Pesher," *RevQ* 3 (1961-1962): 323-64, passim; Cecil Roth, "The Subject Matter of Qumran Exegesis," *VT* 10, no. 1 (Jan. 1960): 51-68, here 64-65; Timothy H. Lim, "Eschatological Orientation and the Alteration of Scripture in the Habakkuk Pesher," *JNES* 49, no. 2 (1990): 185-94; on adaptation of quotations to fit new contexts, see especially Christopher D. Stanley, *Paul and the Language of Scripture: Citation Technique in the Pauline Epistles and Contemporary Literature* (SNTSMS 69; Cambridge: Cambridge University Press, 1992), 291; cf. 335, 337, 342-44. Targum typically proved more expansive (though apparently more in later targumim), and midrash even more so. A primary function of midrash was to reapply texts to contemporary settings (Addison G. Wright, "The Literary Genre Midrash," *CBQ* 28, no. 2 [Apr. 1966]: 105-38, here 133-34).

[67]E.g., Isa 2:2; Ezek 38:16; Hos 3:5; Mic 4:1; Dan 2:28; 11Q13, 2.4; *1 En.* 27:3-4; *T. Iss.* 6:1.

Acts is full of examples of such activities, all of which are meant to characterize the Spirit-empowered eschatological people of God—the Church. (I do, by the way, affirm an end-time turning of the Jewish people to faith in the Messiah, following Paul's imagery of gentile believers being grafted into the covenant and ultimately Jewish believers being regrafted. Because gentile believers are grafted in, however, we already function together with Jewish believers as God's end-time people.)

The universality of the gift is one of its most striking features in this passage. The promise involves sons and daughters, that is, both genders (Acts 2:17).[68] Not surprisingly, Luke tends to pair female prophetesses with male prophets (Luke 2:26-38; Acts 21:9-11; cf. Luke 1:41-45, 67-79); in fact, he actually identifies more prophetesses than prophets.[69] He also mentions the old and the young (Acts 2:17), showing that the gift is for all ages, ranging from the aged widow Anna

---

[68]In Ecuador, women Pentecostals tend to prophesy and have visions more (though prophetic dreams less) than men (Joseph L. Castleberry, "It's Not Just for Ignorant People Anymore: The Future Impact of University Graduates on the Development of the Ecuadorian Assemblies of God" [Ed.D. dissertation, Teachers College, Columbia University, 1999], 142). Historically, many women have found empowerment for their ministry in this text (Janice Capel Anderson, "Reading Tabitha: A Feminist Reception History," 108-44 in *The New Literary Criticism and the New Testament* [ed. Edgar V. McKnight and Elizabeth Struthers Malbon; Valley Forge, PA: Trinity Press International, 1994; Sheffield: JSOT Press, 1994]), particularly prominently in Pentecostalism (see Janet Everts Powers, "'Your Daughters Shall Prophesy': Pentecostal Hermeneutics and the Empowerment of Women," 313-37 in *Globalization of Pentecostalism: A Religion Made to Travel* [ed. Douglas Petersen, et al.; Oxford: Regnum, 1999], 318; Yong, *Spirit Poured*, 190-94; in early Pentecostalism, see Wacker, *Heaven*, 158-65 [though note countervailing cultural and traditional tendencies, 165-76]). For women's ministry in Pentecostalism, see e.g., Powers, "Daughters," 313 (worldwide); Julie Ma, "Asian Women and Pentecostal Ministry," 129-46 in *Asian and Pentecostal: The Charismatic Face of Christianity in Asia* (ed. Allan Anderson and Edmond Tang; foreword by Cecil M. Robeck; Regnum Studies in Mission, AJPS 3; Oxford: Regnum; Baguio City, Philippines: APTS, 2005), 136-42 (the Philippines); Abraham T. Pothen, "Indigenous Cross-Cultural Missions in India and their Contribution to Church Growth: With Special Emphasis on Pentecostal-Charismatic Missions" (Ph.D. Intercultural Studies, Fuller Theological Seminary, School of World Mission, 1990), 191-92, 255 (on Indian missionaries); Ogbu Kalu, *African Pentecostalism: An Introduction* (Oxford: Oxford University, 2008), 161-62 (in Africa).

[69]This does not count the likelihood of the "prophets" in Acts 11:27 being male, since a gender-mixed company would be less likely to travel together in this period (except with relatives; Luke 8:2-3 was exceptional). But of these prophets, only Agabus is given an active role in the narrative (11:28).

(Lk 2:36-37) to the four prophetic young daughters of Philip (21:9),[70] despite ancient Mediterranean society's preference for elders.[71] And further, Luke obliterates the class distinction via Joel's promise that the Spirit will also fall on slaves (Joel 2:29). But he does so in order to remind that all the prophets are God's slaves (Acts 2:18),[72] a common biblical designation for prophets.[73] The fact that they are male and female servants reinforces the transcending of gender barriers.

But perhaps of most immediate importance for Luke's larger narrative in Acts is Joel's "all flesh" (Joel 2:28; Acts 2:17).[74] The point of this phrase, which may have eluded even Peter at this point, will be obvious to Luke's own audience (cf. Luke 2:32; 4:25-27); for them, it harkens back to a programmatic text from Isaiah (cited in Luke 3:6) about all flesh seeing God's salvation. When Peter concludes his sermon with an echo of Isaiah 57:19, indicating that the promise of the Spirit is for all who are "far off," whoever God will call (Acts 2:39),[75] he reinforces God's plan to transcend all cultural barriers to reach all peoples (cf. 22:21). God wants to pour out his Spirit on everyone who will call on his name.

---

[70]"Virgins" probably suggests that they are no older than their teens, since women usually married young and "virgins" thus often functioned as a designation for age. Comparing Mishnaic usage, Hilary Le Cornu with Joseph Shulam, *A Commentary on the Jewish Roots of Acts* (Jerusalem: Nitivyah Bible Instruction Ministry, 2003), 1159, suggests that they had not yet reached puberty.

[71]E.g., Homer *Il.* 1.259; 23.616-23; Livy 5.25.3; 6.24.7; Diogenes Laertius 8.1.22 (Pythagoras); Pliny *Ep.* 8.14.4, 6; *Select Papyri* 3, pp. 476-77, §116; *4 Bar.* 5:20; Sir 8:6; Ps.-Phoc. 220-222; Syriac Menander *Sentences* 11-14; *Epitome* 2-4; *t. Meg.* 3:24; 1 Tim 5:1-2; 1 Pet 5:5. Also in some other societies (e.g., Confucius *Analects* 2.8; 13.20).

[72]Finny Philip, *The Origins of Pauline Pneumatology: The Eschatological Bestowal of the Spirit upon Gentiles in Judaism and in the Early Development of Paul's Theology* (Tübingen: Mohr Siebeck, 2005), 213, suggests that this limits "all flesh" to all *believers*.

[73]2 Kings 9:7, 36; 10:10; 14:25; 17:13, 23; 21:10; 24:2; Ezra 9:11; Isa 20:3; Jer 7:25; 25:4; 26:5; 29:19; 35:15; 44:4; Dan 3:28; 6:20; 9:6, 10; Amos 3:7; Zech 1:6; later, cf. *'Ab. R. Nat.* 37, §95 B.

[74]Cf. e.g., I. Howard Marshall, *The Acts of the Apostles: An Introduction and Commentary* (TNTC; Grand Rapids: Eerdmans, 1980), 73 n. 3; York, *Missions*, 82; Hans F. Bayer, "The Preaching of Peter in Acts," 257-74 in *Witness to the Gospel: The Theology of Acts* (ed. I. Howard Marshall and David Peterson; Grand Rapids: Eerdmans, 1998), 268. Cf. the transcending of the same three barriers, possibly reflecting Joel, in Gal 3:28.

[75]Pao, *Isaianic Exodus*, 230-32.

The Preaching of Pentecost (2:22-40)

Although 2:22-40 is the longest section being covered here, my comments will be relatively brief.   In keeping with the preaching throughout Acts, this passage underlines the sort of Christocentric message that the Spirit particularly empowers. Having quoted the passage from Joel relevant to the current outpouring of the Spirit, Peter now begins to explain the part of it most relevant to his audience, which is, "Whoever calls on the Lord's name will be saved" (2:21).

Joel had announced that, "Whoever calls on the name of YHWH will be delivered" among "those whom the Lord calls" (Joel 2:32). Peter, however, breaks off the quote in 2:21 at, "Whoever calls on the name of the Lord will be saved . . ." and then picks up of the rest of it in 2:39, ". . . as many as the Lord our God shall call." In accord with common midrashic procedure, in the 17 verses between the two, he expounds on the 2:21 portion. Given that the eschatological time (i.e., the time of salvation) has broken in upon them, they must now call on the Lord's name to be saved.[76]

But what is the Lord's name on which the text invites the "whoever" to call? The Hebrew text of Joel 2:32 refers to YHWH, but Jewish people generally avoided pronouncing the divine name. The Greek text, however, uses the normal surrogate for YHWH, namely, "LORD." By linking together texts with common key words (a common Jewish interpretive technique), [77] Peter shows that Jesus is the Lord at the right hand of the Father and hence the Lord on whom they are to call. (This means that Peter is thereby implicitly preaching Jesus's deity.) The apostolic witnesses and the Spirit both testify that Jesus

---

[76]With e.g., Dunn, *Acts*, 27; José Geraldo Costa Grillo, "O discurso de Pedro em Pentecostes: Estudo do gênero literário em Atos 2:14-40," *VS* 7, no. 1 (1997): 37-52; I. Howard Marshall, "Acts," 513-606 in *Commentary on the New Testament Use of the Old Testament* (ed. G. K. Beale and D. A. Carson; Grand Rapids: Baker Academic, 2007), 536, 543; Ernst Haenchen, *The Acts of the Apostles: A Commentary* (Philadelphia: Westminster, 1971), 184 n. 5; Dupont, *Salvation*, 22; Richard F. Zehnle, *Peter's Pentecost Discourse: Tradition and Lukan Reinterpretation in Peter's Speeches of Acts 2 and 3* (SBLMS 15; Nashville: Abingdon, for the Society of Biblical Literature, 1971), 34; Pao, *Isaianic Exodus*, 231-32.

[77]E.g., *Mek. Pisha* 5.103; *Nez.* 10.15-16, 26, 38; 17.17; in this passage, see Richard N. Longenecker, *Biblical Exegesis in the Apostolic Period* (Grand Rapids: Eerdmans, 1975), 97.

has risen, and Peter argues that scripture makes clear the theological implications of this reality for their situation. In Psalm 16:8-11, the risen one (according to Peter's application) is at God's side (2:25-28); in Psalm 110:1, the one at God's right hand is the Lord (2:34-35). They must therefore call on the name of the divine Lord, who is Jesus.[78]

For Peter, this "calling on" the Lord Jesus is not simply reciting a prayer. Rather, it is a public profession that was no less offensive in that culture than John the Baptist immersing fellow Israelites as if they were Gentiles. The concrete expression of "calling on" the Lord that Peter demands is repentance and baptism "in the name of Jesus Christ" (2:38). Baptism in Jesus's name in Acts does not involve a formula that one recites over the person being baptized; the expression "in Jesus's name" accompanies the verb for baptize only when it is in the passive voice (i.e., when people are receiving baptism). It thus involves not the baptizer's formula, but the prayer of the one receiving baptism (cf. 22:16: "be baptized . . . calling on his name"). The Temple Mount was full of baptismal pools for ceremonial washings,79 but this was no ordinary immersion. To publicly accept an immersion like that of Gentiles turning from their former ways constituted a radical declaration of new obedience.

The Purpose of Pentecost (2:41-47)

God poured out the Spirit to empower his people to evangelize cross-culturally, but what was the anticipated outcome of cross-cultural evangelism? God intended to create a new community in which believers would love one another and demonstrate to this age

---

[78]For devotion to Jesus in Luke-Acts, see Larry W. Hurtado, *How on Earth Did Jesus Become a God? Historical Questions about Earliest Devotion to Jesus* (Grand Rapids: Eerdmans, 2005), 160-62; cf. Robert F. O'Toole, *Luke's Presentation of Jesus: A Christology* (SubBi 25; Rome: Editrice Pontificio Istituto Biblico, 2004), passim; C. Kavin Rowe, "Luke and the Trinity: an Essay in Ecclesial Biblical Theology," *SJT* 56, no. 1 (2003): 1-26.

[79]See Bill Grasham, "Archaeology and Christian Baptism," *ResQ* 43, no. 2 (2001): 113-16; for the temple's water supply, see S. Safrai, "The Temple," 865-907 in *The Jewish People in the First Century: Historial Geography, Political History, Social, Cultural and Religious Life and Institutions* (2 vols.; ed. S. Safrai and M. Stern with D. Flusser and W. C. van Unnik; vol. 1: Assen: Van Gorcum & Comp., B.V., 1974; vol. 2: Philadelphia: Fortress, 1976), 884; John McRay, *Archaeology and the New Testament* (Grand Rapids: Baker, 1991), 123.

the very image of the life of his kingdom. The structure of the closing paragraph of the opening section of Acts underlines this purpose of evangelism. Note the following:[80]

- Effective evangelism (2:41)
- Shared worship, meals, and prayer (2:42)
- Shared possessions (2:44-45)
- Shared worship, meals, and prayer (2:46)
- Effective evangelism (2:47)

At the heart of the outcome of new life in the Spirit is not only the Spirit's power and gifting for ministry, but also what we might call (in Paul's language) the Spirit's fruit. Spirit-empowered believers loved each other so much that they valued one another more than they valued their possessions (2:44-45).[81] Just as tongues is repeated at various initial outpourings of the Spirit, this sharing of possessions recurs as a dominant element in the revival in 4:31-35, underlining the importance of this theme (cf. also Lk 12:33; 13:33). Whereas Peter's preaching leads

---

[80]Acts 2:41-47 is the first major summary section; for discussions of such sections, see e.g., H. Alan Brehm, "The Significance of the Summaries for Interpreting Acts," *SWJT* 33, no. 1 (1990): 29-40; S. J. Joubert, "Die gesigpunt van die verteller en die funksie van die Jerusalemgemeente binne die 'opsommings' in Handelinge," *SK* 10, no. 1 (1989): 21-35.

[81]On this passage, see e.g., Thomas Hoyt, Jr., "The Poor in Luke-Acts" (Ph.D. dissertation, Duke University Department of Religion, 1974), 213-22; Alan C. Mitchell, "'Greet the Friends by Name': New Testament Evidence for the Greco-Roman *Topos* on Friendship," 225-62 in *Greco-Roman Perspectives on Friendship* (ed. John T. Fitzgerald; SBLSBS 34; Atlanta: Scholars, 1997), 237-40; on Acts and sharing possessions, see e.g., Luke Timothy Johnson, *The Literary Function of Possessions in Luke-Acts* (SBLDS 39; Missoula, MT: Society of Biblical Literature, 1977); idem, *Sharing Possessions: Mandate and Symbol of Faith* (Philadelphia: Fortress, 1981); Bovon, *Theologian*, 390-96; see more recently John Gillman, *Possessions and the Life of Faith: A Reading of Luke-Acts* (ZSNT; Collegeville, MN: Liturgical, 1991); Kyoung-Jin Kim, *Stewardship and Almsgiving in Luke's Theology* (JSNTSup 155; Sheffield: Sheffield Academic Press, 1998), 218-33; Karris, *Saying*, 84-104. For partial Qumran analogies, see e.g., Joseph A. Fitzmyer, *Essays on the Semitic Background of the New Testament* (2nd ed.; Sources for Biblical Study 5; Missoula, MT: Scholars, 1974), 284-88; David L. Mealand, "Community of Goods at Qumran," *TZ* 31, no. 3 (1975): 129-39; Heinz-Josef Fabry, "Umkehr und Metanoia als monastisches Ideal in der 'Mönchsgemeinde' von Qumran," *ErAuf* 53, no. 3 (1977): 163-80; Hans-Josef Klauck, "Gütergemeinschaft in der Klassischen Antike, in Qumran und im Neuen Testament," *RevQ* 11, no. 1 (1982): 47-79; Reta Halteman Finger, *Of Widows and Meals: Communal Meals in the Book of Acts* (Grand Rapids, Cambridge: Eerdmans, 2007), 146-66.

to many converts on one occasion in 2:41, it is the believing community's lifestyle that leads to continuous conversions in 2:47.

This lifestyle also fits a pattern in Luke's theology of Christian transformation. When the crowds ask Peter what they must do to be saved, he summons them to repent and be baptized in Jesus's name (2:38). But this passage goes on to show us something of what a repentant lifestyle looks like. This fits a pattern of answers to the "What must I do?" question in Luke-Acts.

For instance, when John the Baptist demands the fruits of repentance (Luke 3:8) and the crowds ask what to do, he admonishes that whoever has more than their basic subsistence needs should share the rest with those who have less (Luke 3:11). When a rich ruler asks Jesus what he must do to have eternal life (Luke 18:18), he urges him to donate all his resources to the poor and follow him (Luke 18:22). When the Philippian jailer asks Paul and Silas what he must do to be saved (16:30), they tell him that he must believe in the Lord Jesus (16:31). Lest that seem like a lesser demand than the previous two, consider that the jailer then brings them to his own house and feeds them (16:34), which could have gotten him in serious trouble with the authorities. After all, he had been ordered to securely guard these people who were accused of preaching customs illegal for Philippian citizens to observe (16:21-23).

In Luke-Acts, true conversion involves repentance and commitment to a new Lord. Such commitment also involves commitment to one's new siblings in the new community. As Acts progresses, it becomes clear that this new community does not belong to simply one culture with its table fellowship circumscribed by sacred food customs (10:28; 16:34; 27:35-36).[82] Sometimes, the Christians in Acts do prove reluctant to cross such boundaries (10:28; 11:3; cf. Gal 2:11-14), just as the Pharisees had objected to Jesus's table fellowship

---

[82]The meal in 16:34 cannot have been kosher (cf. Josephus *Life* 13-14), reinforcing the emphasis on crossing cultural barriers there (with Rapske, *Custody*, 215). Common meals in Luke-Acts reveal Christ's family transcending ethnic and cultural barriers (Finger, *Meals*, 280-81, 286; cf. John Ashworth, "Hospitality in Luke-Acts," *BibT* 35, no. 5 (1997): 300-4. The importance of table fellowship may be more intelligible in a modern Asian than a modern western context (Santos Yao, "Dismantling Social Barriers through Table Fellowship, Acts 2:42-47," 29-36 in *Mission in Acts: Ancient Narratives in Contemporary Context* [ed. Robert L. Gallagher and Paul Hertig; AmSocMissS 34; Maryknoll, NY: Orbis Books, 2004], 33-35).

with repenting sinners in Luke 5:30; 7:34; 15:2.[83] But God gives them no rest until he brings them past these barriers.

God is creating a new community that transcends human boundaries. He is empowering his people with the Spirit to cross cultural barriers, to worship him, and to form one new, multi-cultural community of worshipers committed to his Son, Jesus Christ, and to one another.

Conclusion

Acts 1-2 is a pivotal section for Luke-Acts, because it reveals the importance and purpose of the Spirit's empowerment for global mission. The Promise of Pentecost (1:4-8) emphasizes the need for the Spirit, the eschatological character of the Spirit, and the prophetic empowerment dimension of the Spirit. The Preparation for Pentecost (1:12-2:1) involves prayer together and getting ready for God's promise of the Spirit's empowerment in faith. The Proofs of Pentecost (2:2-4) reveal eschatological signs, with tongues-speaking signifying the Spirit's empowerment for cross-cultural witness. The Peoples of Pentecost (2:5-13), though diaspora Jews, foreshadow the Gentile mission and probably evoke a partial inversion of Babel; the mission, this passage reiterates, is for all peoples. The Prophecy of Pentecost (2:17-21) underlines the eschatological, prophetic, and universal character of their empowerment. The Preaching of Pentecost (2:22-40) models the Christocentric message that the Spirit particularly empowers. And lastly, the Purpose of Pentecost (2:41-47) involves the new community that the Spirit-inspired message is meant to form.

The Spirit's empowerment of the Church is central for Luke and is inseparable from the Church's mission in the present age.

---

[83]Pharisees emphasized pure table fellowship (Martin Goodman, *State and Society in Roman Galilee, A. D. 132-212* [Oxford Centre for Postgraduate Hebrew Studies; Totowa, NJ: Rowman & Allanheld, Publishers, 1983], 77). For *Christian* resistance to the gospel in Acts, see Brian Rapske, "Opposition to the Plan and Persecution," 235-56 in *Witness to the Gospel*, 239-45.

Chapter 4

One New Temple in Christ (Eph 2:11-22; Acts 21:27-29; Mk 11:17; Jn 4:20-24)

One striking image in the New Testament is that of a new temple in Christ. Ephesians 2 connects this new temple with the bringing together of Jew and Gentile in shared worship to God. Although the theology of this multi-cultural temple is most obvious in this passage, it develops not only Paul's earlier theology of ethnic reconciliation in Christ (as can be observed, for example, in Romans), but also Jesus's and Paul's own challenges to the traditional temple's ethnic barriers (Mark 11:17; John 4:20-24; Acts 21:27-29).

Traditionally, Christians have defined missions in terms of cross-cultural evangelism and discipleship. The biblical goal of such cross-cultural ministry, however, was never meant to yield a long-range distinction between sending churches and receiving churches. Partnership among churches with reciprocal gifts and responsibilities is a much closer idea (cf. Rom 15:27; 2 Cor 8-9), although the defined roles and differentiation often attached to notions of partnership must be adaptable, pragmatic tools, not inflexible boundaries. The eschatological reality and present ideal in Ephesians 2 point to a more ultimate principle, one of proclaiming an equal citizenship in God's kingdom and a unity in worship that welcomes all contributions without ignoring the diversity of the contributing cultures.

Ephesians 2:11-22 and Paul's Experience with the Divided Temple (Acts 21:27-29)[1]

Paul's image of a temple uniting Jew and Gentile challenged the ethnically segregated reality of the temple standing in his own day. The ancient Israelite temple did not segregate Gentiles from Jews or women from men, but just priests from laity (1 Kings 8:41-43; 2 Chron 6:32-33). By the time of Jesus and Paul, however, Herod's temple did segregate all these groups to fulfill a stricter understanding of purity regulations.[2] The outer court was now divided into the court of Israel (Jewish men only); on a lower level outside it, the court of women (Jewish women only); and on a lower level outside that, the outer court beyond which Gentiles could not pass. Strategically posted signs (attested to by both Josephus and archaeology) warned Gentiles that those who passed this point would be responsible for their own immediate execution.[3]   Although Judeans normally

---

[1] I have treated this subject elsewhere in Craig Keener, "Some New Testament Invitations to Ethnic Reconciliation," *Evangelical Quarterly* 75, no. 3 (2003): 195-213, here 210-13; idem, "The Gospel and Racial Reconciliation," 117-30, 181-90 in *The Gospel in Black & White: Theological Resources for Racial Reconciliation* (ed. Dennis L. Ockholm; Downers Grove, IL: InterVarsity, 1997), 118-22.

[2] See e.g., Josephus *Ant.* 3.318-19; 15.417; *War* 5.194; 6.124-26, 426-27; *m. Kel.* 1:8. Such purity regulations may be partly in mind in Eph 2:15 as it relates to shattering the dividing wall in Eph 2:14.

[3] Josephus *Ant.* 15.417; *War* 5.194; 6.125-26; cf. Philo *Embassy* 212; the inscription in Efrat Carmon, ed., *Inscriptions Reveal: Documents from the Time of the Bible, the Mishna and the Talmud* (trans. R. Grafman; Jerusalem: Israel Museum, 1973), pp. 76, 167-68, §169; G. Adolf Deissmann, *Light from the Ancient East* (Grand Rapids: Baker, 1978), 80-81; comment in Jack Finegan, *The Archeology of the New Testament: The Life of Jesus and the Beginning of the Early Church* (Princeton: Princeton University, 1969), 119-20. Most ancients could not read, but presumably word would spread; many ancient temples had various sorts of purity regulations, some requiring death for violation (e.g., Strabo 14.6.3; Hesiod *Astron.* fig. 3).

were not allowed to execute death sentences directly, violation of their temple constituted the one exception![4]

Both Paul and his audience would have been well-aware of this symbol of Jewish-Gentile division at the very heart of divine worship.[5] In Acts 21:27, some Jewish people from the Roman province of Asia saw Paul exiting the temple. Much of the Jewish community in Ephesus (that province's most prominent city) felt they had reason for animosity against Paul, since he had split their synagogue (19:9) and they had been blamed for a riot in reacting against his monotheistic preaching (19:34-35). Thus, when they saw him in Jerusalem with Trophimus, a Gentile from Ephesus (21:29), and knowing his commitment to Gentiles as well as to Jews, they drew a faulty conclusion—that Paul had violated the temple's sanctity by bringing a Gentile inside (21:28)! A riot quickly ensued;[6] and God ironically used the Roman garrison on the Temple Mount to protect him, even though the garrison commander initially presumed that Paul was the instigator of the unrest.

Paul's ensuing speech to the crowd[7] was in Aramaic, which offered abundant common ground with his audience (e.g., 22:12). Thus they listened patiently to his testimony about Jesus—perhaps because of the culturally sensitive witness of the Jerusalem church (cf. 21:20). Paul could have built on this hearing (as Peter did in 2:37-41) and

---

[4]Cf. Josephus *War* 6.126; *m. Sanh.* 9:6; discussion in Peretz Segal, "The 'Divine Death Penalty' in the Hatra Inscriptions and the Mishnah," *JJS* 40, no. 1 (1989): 46-52.

[5]I cover these observations from Acts in much more detail in my [*Acts: An Exegetical Commentary*, vol. 3.]

[6]Dangerous riots sometimes occurred in the temple (Josephus *War* 2.224-27), requiring extra precautions during the festivals (*War* 5.244); this is probably a festival or just after one (see Acts 20:16).

[7]From the staircase (Acts 21:40) noted in Josephus *War* 5.243-44.

summoned people to repentance. He would not, however, leave out his call to the Gentiles (22:21-22), so the riot resumed.

Why did Paul insist on talking about Gentiles, even when it risked alienating a hostile crowd?[8] Judean nationalism had been on the rise since Judea briefly had its own king (41-44 CE) and suffered abuses under subsequent Roman governors, and revolt against Rome (66-73 CE) was probably less than a decade away. Although the Jerusalem church had successfully identified with their culture in proclaiming Christ to them (21:20), the church did not prophetically warn them that their nationalism was likely leading toward cultural destruction.

The lesson for us is that we should indeed identify with our peoples (cf. 21:26; 1 Cor 9:20-21) but not to the extent of breaking fellowship with believers of other cultures. If Christ is truly our Lord, then we must be loyal to his Body (despite its diversity of languages and customs) more than to any ethnicity. For Paul, as we shall see, the true gospel involved ethnic reconciliation; and someone truly embracing Christ could not hate other peoples. While Paul's provocative message had been rejected, God later

---

[8]Paul did exercise the rhetorical sensitivity to otherwise establish rapport first (as recommended in rhetoric; see e.g., *Rhet. Alex.* 29, 1436b.17-19, 38-40; 1437a.1-1438a.2; 1442a.22-1442b.27).

vindicated that message—and Jesus's warnings (Luke 19:41-44; 21:20-24)—when Jerusalem fell in 70.[9]

Paul's failure to accommodate hatred of Gentiles ironically led to several years in Roman custody. He was held for up to two years in Caesarea (Rome's capital for Judea) then sent on to Rome itself. Paul, from Roman custody (Eph 3:1; 4:1; 6:20),[10] writes to the churches in the Roman province of Asia, starting in Ephesus. (Although Ephesians circulated in Roman Asia beyond Ephesus, that

---

[9]I treat this question more fully in my [*Acts: An Exegetical Commentary*, vol. 3] passim. Since Jesus prophesied this event before 70, this issue differs from the question of Acts' dating; some evangelicals date Acts after 70 (e.g., F. F. Bruce, *The Acts of the Apostles: The Greek Text with Introduction and Commentary* [3rd rev. ed.; Grand Rapids: Eerdmans; Leicester: Apollos, 1990], 18, in contrast to his earlier view; Ben Witherington III, *The Acts of the Apostles: A Socio-Rhetorical Commentary* [Grand Rapids: Eerdmans, 1998], 165-72), others before (e.g., E. M. Blaiklock, *The Acts of the Apostles: An Historical Commentary* [Grand Rapids: Eerdmans, 1959], 16; tentatively, Darrell L. Bock, *Acts* [BECNT; Grand Rapids: Baker Academic, 2007], 25-27).

[10]Many scholars have argued against Pauline authorship; see e.g., Andrew T. Lincoln, *Ephesians* (WBC 42; Dallas: Word, 1990), lix-lxxiii; D. E. Nineham, "The Case Against the Pauline Authorship," 21-35 in *Studies in Ephesians*, ed. F. L. Cross (London: A. R. Mowbray & Co., 1956); C. L. Mitton, *Ephesians*, NCBC (Greenwood, SC: Attic, 1976), 4-11; John C. Kirby, *Ephesians: Baptism and Pentecost. An Enquiry into the Structure and Purpose of the Epistle to the Ephesians* (Montreal: McGill University, 1968), 3-56. But in favor of Pauline authorship, see e.g., Harold W. Hoehner, *Ephesians: An Exegetical Commentary* (Grand Rapids: Baker, 2002), 2-61, 114-30 (thoroughly); J. N. Sanders, "The Case for the Pauline Authorship," 9-20 in *Studies in Ephesians*, ed. Cross; John A. T. Robinson, *Redating the New Testament* (Philadelphia: The Westminster; London: SCM, 1976), 63; Markus Barth, *Ephesians* (2 vols.; AB 34-34A; Garden City, NY: Doubleday & Co., 1974), 1:3-60; cf. A. Van Roon, *The Authenticity of Ephesians* (NovTSup 39; Leiden: E. J. Brill, 1974), 37-44; Henry J. Cadbury, "The Dilemma of Ephesians," *NTS* 5, no. 2 (1959): 91-102. I believe that the style is sufficiently Pauline, if one allows for some "Asianist" rhetoric and his increased skill in using Stoic language (as in Philippians; cf. Acts 19:9), and that Hoehner's argument (favoring Paul's authorship) is compelling.

was probably the center of his audience.[11]) Because both Trophimus' and Paul's accusers were from Ephesus, the believers in Ephesus would know why Paul was writing to them.

For Paul and his audience, there could be no greater symbol of the division between Jew and Gentile than this dividing wall in the temple. Yet he declares that this barrier, established by biblical laws, has been shattered by Jesus Christ—"For he himself is our peace, who forged both Israelite and Gentile into one and abolished the dividing barrier, annulling the enmity . . ." (Eph 2:14-15)! Paul offers this startling claim in a setting where many would have resented it. He was declaring that there was neither Jew nor Gentile in Christ (1 Cor 12:13; Gal 3:28) in a world of mutual hostility between these groups. Sadly, just a few years later, Jews and Syrians began massacring each other in the streets of Caesarea;[12] and less than a decade afterward, Romans devastated Jerusalem, burning its temple and enslaving its survivors.

Yet with a vision to the future, Paul goes on to speak here of a new temple in which Jews and Gentiles together become a holy temple—God's household, the dwelling of the Spirit (2:19-22). Paul's conceptualization of this new

---

[11]For this approach to the circular letter, see e.g., Hoehner, *Ephesians*, 78-79, 144-48; J. Armitage Robinson, *St Paul's Epistle to the Ephesians* (2nd ed.; London: James Clarke & Co. Ltd., 1904), 11; Frank Stagg, *The Book of Acts: The Early Struggle for an Unhindered Gospel* (Nashville, TN: Broadman, 1955), 199; J. Massyngberde Ford, *Revelation* (AB 38; Garden City, NY: Doubleday & Company, 1975), 389; Clinton E. Arnold, *Ephesians: Power and Magic. The Concept of Power in Ephesians in Light of its Historical Setting* (SNTSMS 63; Cambridge: Cambridge University, 1989), 5-6. Manuscripts could also generalize originally more specific addressees; see Harry Y. Gamble, "Canonical Formation of the New Testament," 183-94 in *Dictionary of New Testament Background* (ed. Craig A. Evans and Stanley E. Porter; Downers Grove, IL: InterVarsity, 2000), 186; Lincoln, *Ephesians*, 1-4.

[12]Josephus *War* 2.266-70, 457-58.

temple related concretely to his own situation, but it also reflected antecedent teaching by Jesus himself, who both predicted the temple's destruction[13] and posed theological challenges to the segregation there.

Jesus and the Divided Temple (Mark 11:17; John 4:20-24)

Paul had significant precedent for the connection between the temple and perceptions of Jewish-Gentile separation.[14] As already noted, Herod's temple separated Gentiles (who risked carrying impurity associated with idolatry) from the courts of Jewish women and men. When Jesus overturned the merchants' tables, he challenged the one part of the temple to which Gentiles had access. While one could otherwise doubt a connection between these two features (there being other activities limited to the outer court as well), Mark 11:17 indicates a concern for Gentiles' worship in God's house.[15]

Jesus cried out two texts as he overturned the tables—Isaiah 56:7 and Jeremiah 7:11. The context of Isaiah 56 welcomed Gentiles to worship God, removing their stigma as second-class citizens among the true God's worshipers. In particular, verse 7 declares, "I will bring foreigners to my holy mountain and give them joy in my house for prayer . . .

---

[13]Historically, see Craig S. Keener, *A Commentary on the Gospel of Matthew* (Grand Rapids: Eerdmans, 1999), 560-63, and the many sources cited there; also my forthcoming work on the historical Jesus of the Gospels.

[14]Qumran also spoke of a spiritual temple (e.g., 1QS 8.5-9; Bertril Gärtner, *The Temple and the Community in Qumran and the New Testament: A Comparative Study in the Temple Symbolism of the Qumran Texts and the New Testament* [Cambridge: Cambridge University, 1965], 16-46), but Gentiles were excluded.

[15]Matthew and Luke, laying emphasis instead on the judgment element, omit "Gentiles" here.

because my house will be called a house of prayer for all the nations." Thus, from the outset, God had intended his house to welcome all peoples! Gentiles' restriction to the outer court, however, cannot have encouraged them the way that Isaiah intended.

Jesus blends his reference to Isaiah 56 with another allusion in Jeremiah 7, when he indicates that the Sadducean elite (who currently controlled the temple) had turned it into a "robber's den." This phrase derives from Jeremiah 7:11, in a context emphasizing judgment against the temple. Israel thought that God would never destroy his own temple (7:4). In their estimation (shared with their contemporaries in many surrounding cultures), judgment was not what a god was for. But God challenged their blindness, saying in essence, "Will you mistreat your neighbor and worship other gods, then come into this house that is called by my name and say, 'We are protected'?" (7:5-10). He goes on to warn that they are treating his house like the way robbers treat their lairs—a safe place to store their loot and hide out. But the temple will not protect them; they cannot hide from God's anger there, for he will destroy that temple and banish them from the land (7:12-15).

Jesus does not simply echo texts casually in order to sound biblical, but rather selects these texts deliberately. He pronounced judgment against the temple (Mark 13:1-2), just as Jeremiah did. Overturning merchants' tables offered an even more overt symbol of judgment than had

Jeremiah's smashing of a pot (Jer 19:10-12).[16] Jesus's other teachings[17] suggest that he, like Isaiah, also wanted Gentiles to be welcome in God's eschatological temple.[18] False witnesses seem to have twisted his words about a "new temple" (Mark 14:58; 15:29; cf. Acts 6:14), but John declares that the new temple that Jesus really proclaimed was his body (John 2:19-21).

The Gospels also provide us other indications that Jesus considered a new spiritual temple or at least offered the raw material (cf. e.g., Luke 19:40, 44; 20:17-18)[19] that coalesced into an early Christian consensus about this image (cf. e.g., 1 Cor 3:16; 6:19; 1 Pet 2:4-8; Rev 3:12; 13:6). Clearest among these are Jesus's words to the Samaritan woman in John 4.[20]   In this passage, he seeks a true worshiper of God (John 4:23), hence he "must" pass through Samaria (4:4), even though that route was merely the shortest way, not a strict geographic necessity.[21]

---

[16]Cf. e.g., E. P. Sanders, *Jesus and Judaism* (Philadelphia: Fortress, 1985), 70, 368. Skeptics about Jesus's prediction exercise a double standard against canonical texts; some other Jewish people expected judgment on the temple before the event occurred (*T. Mos.* 6:8-9; *1 En.* 90:28-29; 11QTemple 29:8-10; Josephus *War* 6.301, 304, 306, 309), and others also prophesied Roman conquest before it happened (e.g., 1QpHab 9.6-7). Many less skeptical scholars also point to multiple attestation in favor of Jesus's warning.

[17]See e.g., Michael F. Bird, *Jesus and the Origins of the Gentile Mission* (LNTS 331; London: T&T Clark International, 2006).

[18]On the eschatological temple in Jewish expectation, see Sanders, *Jesus and Judasm*, 77-90.

[19]See my article, "Human Stones in a Greek Setting: Lk 3:8; Matt 3:9; Lk 19:40," *Journal of Greco-Roman Christianity and Judaism*, 6 (2009): 28-36.

[20]I treat this in greater detail, and with further documentation, in Craig S. Keener, *The Gospel of John: A Commentary* (2 vols.; Peabody, MA: Hendrickson, 2003), 611-19.

[21]The verb *dei* refers to divine necessity elsewhere in John (3:7, 14, 30; 4:20, 24; 9:4; 10:16; 12:34; 20:9), and probably bears this sense here (Leon Morris, *The Gospel According to John: The English Text with Introduction, Exposition and Notes* [NICNT; Grand Rapids: Eerdmans, 1971], 255; Raymond E. Brown, *The Gospel According to John* [2 vols.; AB 29-29A; Garden City, NY: Doubleday & Company, 1966-1970], 1:169; J. Ramsey Michaels, *John* [GNC; San Francisco: Harper & Row, 1984], 59). Samaria was the preferred route (Josephus *War* 2.232; *Ant.* 10.118), but "necessary" only if one required haste (*Life* 269), which Jesus apparently did not (John 4:40).

Jesus crosses multiple barriers to talk with this woman. First, he crosses a gender barrier. Strict Jewish pietists did not wish to be seen talking alone with a woman. In their estimation, not only might this arouse temptation, but it might hurt one's reputation for piety.[22] Thus the text notes that Jesus's disciples were "surprised" to find him speaking with a woman, although it also implies that they knew him well enough not to question him (4:27).

Second, as with tax collectors and sinners in the other Gospels, Jesus crosses a moral barrier that his strictest contemporaries normally would not have. In this culture, most women came to the well together. That this woman came separately and at the hottest time of day (about the sixth hour, 4:6)[23] made it obvious that she was not welcome in the company of the other women.[24] Shockingly, Jesus asks her for a drink (4:7), something normal religious Jewish men would not do. Jewish law treated Jewish women as unclean one week of every month, but strict Jewish pietists viewed Samaritan women as unclean every week of every month (immoral or not)![25]

Also, pietists would have resented the setting's ambiguity, because wells were notorious. It was at wells

---

[22]E.g., Sir 9:9; 42:12; *m. Ab.* 1:5; *Ket.* 7:6; *t. Shab.* 1:14; *b. Ber.* 43b, bar. More widely, see e.g., Euripides *Electra* 343-44; Livy 34.2.9, 18 (though most Romans were more progressive). In the Middle East today, Carol Delaney, "Seeds of Honor, Fields of Shame," 35-48 in *Honor and Shame and the Unity of the Mediterranean* (ed. David D. Gilmore; AAAM 22; Washington, D.C.: American Anthropological Association, 1987), 41, 43.

[23]E.g., Sophocles *Antig.* 416; Apollonius Rhodius 2.739; 4.1312-13; Ovid *Metam.* 1.591-92; *Jos. Asen.* 3:2/3:3. People thus normally broke from work and found shade at this time (e.g., Columella *Trees* 12.1; Longus 2.4; Ovid *Metam.* 3.143-54). It aroused thirst (Livy 44.36.1-2; Longus 3.31), also relevant here (John 4:7).

[24]Cf. e.g., Brown, *John*, 1:169.

[25]*M. Nid.* 4:1; *Toh.* 5:8; *t. Nid.* 5:1; see comments in David Daube, *The New Testament and Rabbinic Judaism* (Peabody, MA: Hendrickson Publishers, n.d.; London: University of London, 1956), 373.§19.

that Isaac's steward met Rebekah (Gen 24:11, 15-19), Jacob met Rachel (Gen 29:10), and Moses met Zipporah (Exod 2:15-17). Other sources show us that some people considered a well an appropriate place to find a mate.[26] When Jesus asks this woman to bring her husband (John 4:16), she apparently assumes that he is questioning whether she is married, and she responds that she is not (4:17)—in other words, that she is available. At this point, Jesus identifies the real issue, which was her not being married to the man she's living with (4:18). Thus her further response was that Jesus must be a prophet (4:19). One would not have to be a prophet merely to discern that she had a bad reputation, since her coming to the well alone suggested that. Yet Jesus further revealing that she had been married five times before and was not married to her current boyfriend was not the sort of thing a stranger could have known.

Third, Jesus crosses the cultural and ethnic barrier. As we already learned in 4:9, Jews did not deal with Samaritans—and vice versa. Now the woman claims that Jesus is a prophet. As best as we can reconstruct on the basis of later Samaritan traditions, however, Samaritans did not believe in regular prophets, apart from an end-time prophet like Moses.[27] By calling this Jew a prophet, she implicitly acknowledges that the Jewish people rather than the Samaritans are right about God (as Jesus reaffirms in 4:22).

---

[26]Arrian *Alex.* 2.3.4; perhaps *Lam. Rab.* 1:1, §19.
[27]F. F. Bruce, *New Testament History* (Garden City, NY: Doubleday & Company, 1972), 37-38; idem, *The Time is Fulfilled* (Grand Rapids: Eerdmans, 1978), 39. Josephus' Samaritan prophet on Mount Gerizim (*Ant.* 18.85-86) possibly fits this expectation.

When she goes on to say, "Our ancestors worshiped at this mountain" (Mount Gerizim,[28] in full view of the well), "but you Jews worship in Jerusalem," we might suppose that she is trying to change the subject in order to evade the issue of her immorality. But such a cultural reading is far from how Samaritans would have understood it. If Jesus is a prophet, then her entire religious worldview must be reconstructed.

The most fundamental point of contention between Jews and Samaritans was their respective holy sites. This is evident already in the verb tenses she employs—"Your ancestors worshipped (aorist) . . . , but you Jews worship" (present) . . ." Jews had destroyed the Samaritans' temple on Mount Gerizim about 150 years earlier.[29] Samaritans would never have been able to destroy Jerusalem's Temple Mount, but they had once desecrated it[30] and continue to ridicule it.[31] Samaritans were now barred from Jerusalem's temple.[32] Thus, if the Jewish people are right and the Samaritans wrong, how can this woman worship God?

---

[28]For Samaritan emphasis on Mount Gerizim, see Josephus *Ant.* 18.85-87; *War* 3.307-15; *t. A.Z.* 3:13; John Bowman, *Samaritan Documents Relating to Their History, Religion & Life* (POTTS 2; Pittsburgh, PA: Pickwick, 1977), 14.

[29]Josephus *War* 1.63-66; *Ant.* 13.255-56. Scholars have cited possible archaeological evidence for its destruction; see Robert J. Bull, "Field Report XII," *BASOR* 180 (Dec. 1965): 37-41, here 41; Finegan, *Archeology*, 35; Howard Clark Kee, "Tell-Er-Ras and the Samaritan Temple," *NTS* 13, no. 4 (1967): 401-2; G. G. Garner, "The Temples of Mt. Gerizim. Tell er Ras—Probable Site of the Samaritan Temple," *Buried History* 11, no. 1 (1975): 33-42; Benedikt Schwank, "Grabungen auf 'diesem Berg' (Joh 4,20-21). Der archäologische Beitrag," *BK* 47, no. 4 (1992): 220-21. Others, however, find this more questionable; see Robert T. Anderson, "The Elusive Samaritan Temple," *BA* 54, no. 2 (1991): 104-7; but cf. John McRay, "Archaeology and the NT," 93-100 in *Dictionary of NT Background*, 96.

[30]Josephus *Ant.* 18.29-30.

[31]See e.g., *Gen. Rab.* 32:10; 81:3; cf. Luke 9:51-53.

[32]Josephus *Ant.* 18.30. This exclusion began in the time of Coponius (*Ant.* 18.29), who was governor from 6-9 CE.

Jesus responds that the true site of worship is neither in Jerusalem nor on Mount Gerizim. Rather, the true place is in Spirit and in truth (possibly a hendiadys for "in the Spirit of truth").[33] That is, no physical location defines where God is to be worshipped; what matters is Spirit-empowered worship (4:24).[34] God is so great that no worship of him is adequate unless God's own Spirit births it. The true temple is us dwelling in God and God dwelling in us (cf. John 14:23). Even in Revelation, where we might expect an eschatological temple like the one described in Ezekiel 40-48, we find something better, not worse, than Ezekiel's vision.[35] The entire New Jerusalem, which is shaped like the Holy of Holies, has no need of a temple, for God dwells with all his people in all the city. God himself and the Lamb are its temple (Rev 21:22).

Because the true temple is one in the Spirit, Jesus crossed those three barriers to make this woman a true worshiper of God. Because true worship is not limited to any geographic location or ethnicity or culture, we must cross every barrier to introduce people to new life (hence true worship of God) in the Spirit.

---

[33] With Brown, *John*, 1:180.
[34] Cf. Phil 3:3; discussion in Keener, *John*, 615-19.
[35] See Craig Keener, *Revelation* (NIVAC; Grand Rapids: Zondervan, 1999), 497, especially 504.

Paul's Theology of Multi-Cultural Unity in Christ (Romans)[36]

In Ephesians, Paul's vision of a new spiritual temple is no afterthought to his theology; in earlier letters he had already addressed all believers as a spiritual temple (1 Cor 3:16; 6:19; 2 Cor 6:16) and those who offer spiritual worship (Rom 12:1). Even more critically, the bringing together of Jews and Gentiles had always been a dominant element in his preaching. In the United States, where in some locations blacks and whites once had to eat at different lunch counters, I like to remark that Paul once challenged Peter at a segregated lunch counter (Gal 2:11-14).

Paul is most explicit about this perspective in Romans, probably because the church in Rome had special problems surrounding it. Following Claudius' edict (probably c. AD 49),[37] many Jewish Christians left Rome (Acts 18:1-3); but when Claudius died a few years later, some returned (Rom

---

[36] I address this theme in Romans in more detail in Keener, "Gospel and Reconciliation," 122-25; idem, "Invitations," 208-10; also my *Romans, New Covenant Commentary Series* (Eugene, OR: Wipf & Stock, 2009).

[37] Suetonius *Claud.* 25.4. For the date, see e.g., Arthur Darby Nock, "Religious Developments from the Close of the Republic to the Death of Nero," 465-511 in *The Augustan Empire: 44 B.C. – A.D. 70*, vol. 10 in *The Cambridge Ancient History* (12 vols., ed. S. A. Cook, F. E. Adcock and M. P. Charlesworth; Cambridge: University Press, 1966), 500; Rudolf Brändle and Ekkehard W. Stegemann, "The Formation of the First 'Christian Congregations' in Rome in the Context of the Jewish Congregations," 117-27 in *Judaism and Christianity in First-Century Rome* (ed. Karl P. Donfried and Peter Richardson; Grand Rapids: Eerdmans, 1998), 125-26; George Howard, "The Beginnings of Christianity in Rome: A Note on Suetonius, Life of Claudius XXV.4," *ResQ* 24, no. 3 (1981): 175-77; Stanley E. Porter, "Chronology, New Testament," 201-8 in *Dictionary of New Testament Background*, 206; Robert O. Hoerber, "The Decree of Claudius in Acts 18:2," *CTM* 31, no. 11 (1960): 690-94; Jacob Jervell, *Die Apostelgeschichte* (KEKNT 17; Göttingen: Vandenhoeck & Ruprecht, 1998), 458; Lo Lung-Kwong, *Paul's Purpose in Writing Romans: The Upbuilding of A Jewish and Gentile Christian Community in Rome* (Jian Dao DS 6, Bible and Literature 4; Hong Kong: Alliance Bible Seminary, 1998), 78-82; Peter Lampe, *From Paul to Valentinus: Christians at Rome in the First Two Centuries* (ed. Marshall D. Johnson; trans. Michael Steinhauser; Minneapolis: Fortress, 2003), 11-16.

16:3). Many or most scholars believe that the consequent influx of Jewish believers into what had for several years been a largely Gentile movement in Rome set the stage for the clash of cultures there.[38] I agree that this scenario is very likely, but we may be even more certain about Paul's solution, since it remains explicit in the letter itself, in which he goes out of his way to emphasize that salvation is for both Jew and Gentile (e.g., 1:16; 10:11-13). The body of his letter climaxes with scriptural proofs for Jews and Gentiles worshiping God together (15:6-12).[39]

Paul constructs all of Romans to advance this theme. Jewish hearers[40] would agree with his verdict that the Gentiles are lost (1:18-32), but he uses this same verdict to establish in the next two chapters that Jews are also lost (2:1 through 3:23). Thus, Paul argues, all must come to God the same way—i.e., through Jesus Christ (3:24-31). Some Jewish people would have demurred, holding that they were saved because they were chosen in Abraham![41] Paul responds that, far from being able to depend on

---

[38]E.g., A. Andrew Das, *Paul and the Jews* (Peabody: Hendrickson, 2003), 53-61; James D. G. Dunn, *Romans* (2 vols.; WBC 38A, B; Dallas: Word, 1988), 1:liii; Lung-Kwong, *Purpose*, 78-82; Douglas J. Moo, *The Epistle to the Romans* (Grand Rapids, Cambridge: Eerdmans, 1996), 5; Thomas R. Schreiner, *Romans* (BECNT; Grand Rapids: Baker, 1998), 12-14, 797-98; Thomas H. Tobin, *Paul's Rhetoric in Its Contexts: The Argument of Romans* (Peabody, MA: Hendrickson, 2004), 35-41; A. Katherine Grieb, *The Story of Romans: A Narrative Defense of God's Righteousness* (Louisville, London: Westminster John Knox, 2002), 7.

[39]For Paul seeking to reconcile Jewish and Gentile believers in Rome, see e.g., W. S. Campbell, "Why Did Paul Write Romans?" *Expository Times* 85, no. 9 (1974) 264-69; Bruce Chilton, *Judaic Approaches to the Gospels* (USFISFCJ, vol. 2; Atlanta: Scholars Press, 1994), 222-24; Schreiner, *Romans*, 19-21; Lung-Kwong, *Purpose*, 413-14.

[40]Technically, most of Romans' audience is ethnically Gentile (cf. 1:5, 13; 11:13), though they will identify with the Jewish roots of their faith.

[41]Neh 9:7; Mic 7:20; E. P. Sanders, *Paul and Palestinian Judaism: A Comparison of Patterns of Religion* (Philadelphia: Fortress, 1977), 87-101; Marcus J. Borg, *Conflict, Holiness & Politics in the Teachings of Jesus* (SBEC 5; New York: Edwin Mellen, 1984), 207.

ancestral merit, they must follow Abraham's model, which is justification through faith alone (4:1-5:11). Moreover, if they wished to appeal to their ancestry in Abraham, he reminds them of everyone's common ancestry in Adam, who introduced sin (5:12-21).[42]

Jewish people might object that the law gave them a righteousness that unconverted Gentiles could not possess and (close to Paul's concern here) that converted Gentiles could acquire only with difficulty. Many sages felt most Jews usually kept all 613 commandments that Jewish tradition found in the Torah, whereas most Gentiles could not even maintain the seven commandments that Jewish tradition attributed to Noah. But Paul insists that the law, although it was meant to bring life, actually facilitated his death because it could not transform him (7:7-25).[43] The law could inform him about righteousness but could transform him only if written in his heart by the Spirit (8:2; cf. Ezek 36:26-27; 2 Cor 3:3-6).

Now in Romans 9 through 11, Paul comes to the heart of his argument about the relation between Jew and Gentile. Jewish people believed that they were chosen in Abraham, but Paul insists that, with respect to salvation, God is not bound to choose on the basis of ethnicity. Indeed, he warns that "not all Israel's descendants are Israel" nor are all Abraham's descendants counted as his

---

[42]Jewish people agreed that Adam introduced sin and death (*4 Ezra* 3:7; 4:30; *2 Bar.* 17:2-3; 23:4; 48:42-45; 56:5-6; *L.A.E.* 44:3-4; *Sipre Deut.* 323.5.1; 339.1.2), but many believed that his descendants also replicated the sin (*4 Ezra* 3:21; *2 Bar.* 18:1-2; 54:15, 19; cf. *4 Ezra 4 Ezra* 7:118-26).

[43]I agree with most scholars that the point of Rom 7 is life under the law more generally, not Paul's personal autobiography, but believe that Paul's own background enables and informs his description. The point would not differ for our purposes in any case.

children (9:6-7). Abraham had two sons while Sarah remained alive—Isaac and Ishmael—yet only one received the promise (9:7-8), although both were blessed. Likewise, Isaac had two sons—Esau and Jacob—but only one received the promise (9:10-13). In view of this pattern, how could Jewish people assume that they automatically belonged to the saving covenant based on their ethnicity?

But lest we think that Paul lectures only the minority of Jewish believers in Jesus involved with the Roman church, he decisively challenges the now-complacent and dominant Gentile believers as well. Not only is there still a remnant of Jewish believers (11:1-5) and a long-range hope for the Jewish people submitting to Jesus (11:12, 15, 26-27),[44] but also Gentile believers are merely grafted as proselytes into Israel's heritage (11:17-21).[45] As God used Israel's disobedience to afford opportunity for Gentiles' repentance before the end of the age, he also uses Gentiles' obedience through Christ to provoke Israel's jealousy that

---

[44]The sense of "Israel" in the immediate context of 11:26 seems ethnic rather than spiritual; cf. Johannes Munck, *Christ & Israel: An Interpretation of Romans 9-11* (Philadelphia: Fortress, 1967), 136; George E. Ladd, "Israel and the Church," *Evangelical Quarterly* 36 (1964): 206-13.

[45]For Gentile converts as proselytes here, see Terence L. Donaldson, "'Riches for the Gentiles' (Rom 11:12): Israel's Rejection and Paul's Gentile Mission," *JBL* 112, no. 1 (1993): 81-98; idem, "Israelite, Convert, Apostle to the Gentiles: The Origin of Paul's Gentile Mission," 62-84 in *The Road from Damascus: The Impact of Paul's Conversion on His Life, Thought, and Ministry* (ed. Richard N. Longenecker; Grand Rapids: Eerdmans, 1997), 81-82; idem, *Paul and the Gentiles: Remapping the Apostle's Convictional World* (Minneapolis: Fortress, 1997), 230-47; also Richard B. Hays, *The Conversion of the Imagination: Paul as Interpreter of Israel's Scripture* (Grand Rapids: Eerdmans, 2005): 5.

eschatological expectations about Gentiles are being fulfilled through Christ (11:13-14).[46]

Having established the theological groundwork, Paul now turns to the practical demand that follows from these observations—i.e., believers need to serve one another (12:9-15), for the heart of the law is loving one another (13:8-10). On a practical level, this teaching especially meant that Gentile believers must not look down on Jewish people's food customs or holy days (Rom 14:1-15:6), which ancient sources show Roman Gentiles frequently did.[47] Rather, Paul urges unity in Christ that welcomes, not suppresses, the diversity of our cultures.

Paul concludes that argument by citing scriptures for Jews and Gentiles united in common worship of Israel's true God (15:6-12) then offers the following examples of Jewish-Gentile cooperation:

- Jesus, although Jewish, became a minister to the Gentiles (15:8-9).
- Paul, a Jewish missionary, evangelizes Gentiles (15:18-24).
- Paul brings an offering from the mixed diaspora churches to the needy believers in Jerusalem (15:25-27) and invites the Gentile Roman believers to partner with him in prayer (15:30) and support (15:24, 28).

---

[46]See discussion in Mark D. Nanos, *The Mystery of Romans: The Jewish Context of Paul's Letter* (Minneapolis: Fortress, 1996), 249-50; see also Craig S. Keener, "Interdependence and Mutual Blessing in the Church," in *Introduction to Messianic Judaism: Its Ecclesial Context and Biblical Foundations* (ed. David Rudolph and Joel Willitts; Grand Rapids: Zondervan, 2013), 187-95.

[47]See e.g., Juvenal *Sat.* 14.96-106.

- Paul exhorts both Jewish and Gentile believers to beware of those who cause division among them (16:17).[48]

From start to finish, a central concern of Paul in writing Romans appears to be the uniting of believers of different backgrounds.

Personal note. When I was going through the deepest crisis of my life since my conversion, an African-American family basically adopted me into their family and circle of churches and nurtured me back to wholeness. African-Americans had survived slavery and countless other trials and had learned how to depend on God in ways that I had not discovered in the white church circles of which I had usually been a part. Since 1991 I have been a minister in a largely African-American church movement.[49] My wife, who is from the Congo in Central Africa, survived 18 months as a refugee during an ethnic war in her country. Over that time, she and her family showed love to people from the other side of the war, including providing for a foreign mercenary (working for that other side) who had been captured and abused.[50] We have observed that

---

[48]Perhaps even over food (16:18). Nevertheless, "belly" was used widely in moralistic literature for any uncontrolled passions; see e.g., 3 Macc 7:11; Philo *Spec. Laws* 1.148, 192, 281; 4.91; further sources in Keener, *Matthew*, 342; for "slave of the belly," as here, see e.g., Maximus of Tyre *Or.* 25.6; Achilles Tatius 2.23.1; Philostratus *V.A.* 1.7.

[49]On the story, see e.g., Lynette Blair Mitchell, "Charismatic Scholar Targets Racism," *Charisma* (June 1996): 28, 30; Gayle White, "Colorblind Calling," *The Atlanta Journal & Constitution* (Nov. 3, 1991): M1, 4; Flo Johnston, "Ordination will cross racial lines," *Religious News Service* (e.g., in *Chicago Tribune*, Aug. 9, 1991, secton 2.9).

[50]See e.g., Craig Keener and Médine Moussounga Keener, "Reconciliation for Africa: Resources for Ethnic Reconciliation" (Bukuru: Africa Christian Textbooks, 2006), 12; Craig Keener and Médine Moussounga Keener, *Impossible Love* (Grand Rapids: Chosen, 2016).

Christ's love must transcend ethnic boundaries, no matter what the cost.

Eschatological Unity and God's Temple (Rev 5:9; 7:9)

The image of united, multi-cultural worship to God continues into the latest parts of the New Testament, the closing witness of the first apostolic church. Thus the 'furniture' that Revelation depicts in heaven evokes that of the biblical temple—the ark (Rev 11:19), an altar of sacrifice (6:9), an altar of incense (8:3-5), a sea (4:6; 15:2; cf. 1 Kings 7:23-25), lamps (Rev 4:5), and even harps (14:2; 15:2). Indeed, it is called both a tabernacle (Rev 13:6; 15:5) and a temple (14:15, 17; 15:5-8; 16:1, 17). So what does one do in a temple? In particular, one worships. Whereas the scenes of earth in Revelation involve judgment (e.g., chs. 6; 8-9; 16) or the worship of the beast (13:4, 8, 12, 15; 14:11; 16:2; 19:20; cf. 9:20), the scenes of heaven involve worshipping God and the Lamb (4:8-10; 5:9-14; 7:11; 11:1, 16; 14:7; 19:4).[51]

Likewise, in the eternal future, the very shape of the New Jerusalem evokes (as noted earlier) the Holy of Holies (21:16; cf. 1 Kings 6:20). One would normally not expect a city to be over 2,000 kilometers high, but its equal length, breadth, and height reinforces the allusion to the Holy of Holies. When God promises that he will dwell among his people there (21:3), he portrays the city not only as a temple, but also as the Holy of Holies itself! Thus the eternal future, involving 'heaven on earth' so to speak,

---

[51]See also Keener, *Revelation*, 91-92.

continues the worship that Revelation reveals already in heaven (22:3). Although the New Jerusalem is for all believers, it is founded on the twelve tribes of Israel and the twelve apostles of the Lamb (21:12, 14).

One of Revelation's scenes of worship shows that the multi-cultural multitude has been grafted into Israel's heritage (7:9-17). Although this multitude is comprised of members from all peoples (7:9),[52] Jesus's followers are depicted in language evoking prophetic promises to Israel, because devotion to Israel's true king rather than ethnicity determines one's status in God's covenant (cf. 2:9; 3:9). Thus, they neither hunger nor thirst nor suffer from the sun, but the Lamb leads them to springs of water (7:16). Revelation's language here mirrors Isaiah 49:10, where God would protect his people from hunger, thirst, and the sun and would lead them to springs of water. In Revelation 7:17, the Lamb wipes away the tears of his followers; and in Isaiah 25:8, at the resurrection God would wipe away his people's tears. By the way this passage reframes Old Testament prophecies, it emphasizes that Jesus is God and that his followers from all nations are together God's people.

This scene immediately follows another vision in which God has 144,000 servants from Israel's twelve tribes. Since scripture predicts the turning of the Jewish people to Christ in the end time (Rom 11:26-27), we cannot rule out the possibility that this eschatological event is the point of this

---

[52]This echoes Nebuchadnezzar's empire (e.g., Dan 3:7, 31; 5:19; 6:25; 7:14; esp. 3:4), but God's kingdom would supplant all worldly empires (2:44-45), and will include representatives from all peoples (7:13-14; see Richard Bauckham, *The Climax of Prophecy: Studies on the Book of Revelation* [Edinburgh: T. & T. Clark, 1993], 326-29).

image in Revelation. Sometimes in scripture, however, a second vision or dream simply re-articulates the point of the first one (e.g., Gen 37:7, 9; 40:1-7), and that may be the case here.[53]

We have already seen that 7:9-17 portrays believers from all nations as part of God's people. So what is the likelihood that this is the case for the 144,000? We do know that Revelation portrays all believers as spiritually Jewish, grafted into Israel's heritage (e.g., 1:20;[54] 2:9; 3:9). Moreover, the 144,000 is the number of God's servants (7:3-4), which elsewhere in Revelation involves the saved (1:1; 10:7; 11:18; 19:2, 5; 22:3, 6). The seal on them connects them with all believers (3:12; 22:4; cf. 2 Cor 1:22; Eph 1:13; 4:30; Ezek 9:4; *Ps. Sol.* 15:6-9). Further, John's vision omits the tribe of Dan from the list of tribes, which is a curious omission if he intends the designation literally, since in Ezekiel the tribe of Dan receives the first eschatological allotment (Ezek 48:1).

Most importantly, Revelation reuses these numbers later. Although translations sometimes obscure the figures,

---

[53]With most commentators, e.g., G. B. Caird, *A Commentary on the Revelation of Saint John the Divine* [HNTC; New York: Harper & Row, 1966], 94-95; Mathias Rissi, *Time and History: A Study on the Revelation* (trans. Gordon C. Winsor; Richmond, VA: John Knox, 1966), 89, 110; Robert H. Mounce, *The Book of Revelation* (NICNT; Grand Rapids: Eerdmans, 1977], 168-70; George R. Beasley-Murray, *The Book of Revelation* (NCBC; Greenwood, SC: Attic; London: Marshall, Morgan & Scott, 1974], 140; Bauckham, *Climax*, 399; Alan F. Johnson, *Revelation* (Expositor's Bible Commentary; Zondervan, 1996), 85; J. Ramsey Michaels, *Revelation* (IVPNTC; Downers Grove, IL: InterVarsity, 1997), 113; Gregory K. Beale, *The Book of Revelation: A Commentary on the Greek Text* (Grand Rapids: Eerdmans, 1999), 412-23. I address this in Keener, *Revelation*, 230-33.

[54]Lampstands were the most pervasive symbol for Judaism in the Roman empire; see e.g., *CIJ* 1:8, §4; 1:16, §14; 2:12, §743; 2:32, §771 and passim through 2:53, §801 (*CIJ* altogether contains about 200 examples); Harry J. Leon, *The Jews of Ancient Rome* (Philadelphia: The Jewish Publication Society of America, 1960), 49, 196-97; Erwin R. Goodenough, *Jewish Symbols in the Greco-Roman Period* (13 vols.; New York: Pantheon Books for Bollingen Foundation, 1953-1965), 12:79-83.

the New Jerusalem is 12,000 stadia (about 1,500 miles or 2,400 kilometers) cubed, with a wall of some 144 cubits (over 200 feet or nearly 80 meters) (21:16-17). A wall of that size is utterly disproportionate to a city that's 1,500 miles (2,400 kilometers) long, wide, and tall.[55] But Revelation elsewhere informs us that the measurements involve the people, not just the place (11:1). The New Jerusalem is the city of God for the people of God, a city whose very dimensions evoke the 144,000. When John saw the Lamb's followers standing on Mount Zion (14:1), it was likely because they symbolized the citizens of the new Zion.

Revelation speaks of two cities. One is the city of the present evil empires (this present world), portrayed as Babylon the prostitute and decorated with gold and pearls (17:3-5).[56] Those without faith to await the future city settle for the prostitute. But those who keep themselves chaste, such as the 144,000 in 14:4, await a better city—the New Jerusalem (the bride of Christ), whose streets are gold and whose gates pearls (21:2, 10-11, 18-21). This world is nothing compared to the world to come!

Ancient cities always had temples, but John says of the New Jerusalem, "I saw no temple there . . ." (21:16).[57] The

---

[55]To compensate, some translations assign the cubit measure to the wall's thickness (see Ezek 41:9, 12; see Aune, *Revelation* [3 vols.; WBC 52, 52b, 52c; Dallas: Word, 1997], 1162), but this is still utterly disproportionate from an ancient or even modern engineering standpoint.

[56]I do agree with those who see Babylon through the lens of Rome, because Rome was the "Babylon" of John's day (having destroyed Jerusalem like Babylon of old, and becoming even a Jewish cipher for Rome; see 1 Pet 5:13; *Sib. Or.* 5.143, 159-61; *4 Ezra* 3:1-2, 28; *2 Bar.* 11:1-2; 67:7). But the very use of the symbolic title "Babylon" also looks beyond Rome, epitomizing more generally evil empire (i.e., what is analogous to Babylon).

[57]This contrasts starkly with ancient Jewish expectations (*Jub.* 1:27-29; *1 En.* 90:28-29; *Sib. Or.* 3.702-6; *m. Ab.* 5:20; *Taan.* 4:8; fully Charles H. Talbert, *The Apocalypse: A Reading of the Revelation of John* [Louisville, KY: Westminster John Knox, 1994], 102).

New Jerusalem itself, and New Jerusalemites (cf. 3:12), are God's temple (21:3). He dwells in us, and we dwell in him (21:22). In a city whose gates were named for the twelve tribes and its foundation stones for the twelve apostles, Jew and Gentile together worship God and the Lamb in the fullness of their glory forever and ever. The city of God for the people of God includes all who follow the Lamb.

Conclusion

How central is our unity in Christ? It is central enough to transcend all other loyalties, so that loyalty to Christ as Lord entails loyalty to one another as God's family, above all ethnic, cultural, and earthly kinship connections. It is central enough that Paul repeatedly emphasizes it as a necessary corollary of the gospel. It is central enough that the worship that God desires is a united worship of believers from many different peoples and languages. We are different, bringing diverse cultural gifts; but we are one, for God (the Lord whom we worship) is One.[58]

---

[58]I evoke here the Shema (Deut 6:4), a fundamental principle of Judaism (cf. e.g., *Let. Aris.* 131-32; *m. Ber.* 1:1 and passim; *Tam.* 5:1; *Sipre Deut.* 31.4.1; William Oscar Emil Oesterley, *The Jewish Background of the Christian Liturgy* (Oxford: Clarendon, 1925), 42-46; Ephraim E. Urbach, *The Sages: Their Concepts and Beliefs* (2d ed.; 2 vols.; trans. Israel Abrahams; Jerusalem: Magnes, Hebrew University, 1979), 1:19-36, 400-2) and a basic presupposition of NT theology (Mark 12:29; Rom 3:30; 1 Cor 8:6; Jas 2:19).

Chapter 5

Between Asia and Europe: Post-Colonial Mission in Acts 16:8-10

S ome observers in recent centuries have misunderstood Christianity as being a European movement. However, first-century observers could not have imagined this misconception, for they viewed Judea and Galilee, their larger province of Syria, and what we call Asia Minor as parts of Asia. Moreover, the one scene in which Acts could possibly be interpreted as describing the entrance of the gospel into Europe clearly shows it as originating from western Asia.

The traditional division of these two continents has always been arbitrary. Greeks counted themselves as in Europe and distinguished themselves from Asian peoples to their east and, later, Africa to their south. Nevertheless, the division appeared significant to the many people in the Roman Empire who had accepted Greek categories, and Greeks treated the Troad as the traditional entry point into "Asia" (i.e., the world to the west of the Greek homeland).[1]

Although Luke does not explicitly use the language of either Europe or Asia here, even a minimally culturally literate Greek audience would understand Troas' strategic role in these boundaries. This site further evoked both the legendary conflict between the Achaians and Trojans and the Persian conquests of Alexander, both of which Greeks conceptualized as European invasions of Asia. By contrast, Rome detested 'Asian religions' like Judaism. It is thus possible that Luke's original audience[2] would envision a reverse

---

[1]See discussion in Glenn J. Usry and Craig S. Keener, *Black Man's Religion: Can Christianity be Afrocentric?* (Downers Grove: InterVarsity, 1996).

[2]I envision his ideal audience as from somewhere in the Greek-speaking eastern Mediterranean world, especially in the north or west Aegean region. If the audience was from the eastern Aegean, they would have viewed themselves as part of Asia.

movement of an Asian faith into Europe in what we might today call anti-colonial terms.[3] Although the Alexander allusion remains less than certain, for an audience in the Roman Empire, the Asian geographic provenance of the gospel would be beyond dispute.

Troas' Location and Importance

After a long journey from the interior of southern Asia Minor, Paul and his companions reached Alexandria Troas. Because Troas was not far from the coast, their "descent" to it in Acts 16:8 is aptly phrased.[4] Although not yet certain of where to proceed, they probably entered Troas deliberately. It had a large artificial harbor that made it strategic for travel between the east and the west.[5] This strategic location suggests that Paul and Silas may have hoped to sail from there. Thus, it was not likely a destination reached accidentally from their previous locations (16:6-8).[6] That is, these missionaries likely did not intend Troas as their final destination.

Although Alexandria Troas in Paul's day was still overshadowed by the reputation of nearby Troy (Ilium) of the legendary past, it was hardly forgettable on its own merit. In the Hellenistic and Roman periods, Alexandria Troas constituted the largest city in the Troad (i.e., the region of Troy).[7] While most of the city still remains unexcavated, it is thought to cover over 1,000 acres, with its ancient walls once five miles around.[8] The limited archaeological data support ancient

---

[3]Scholars emphasizing post-colonial readings should find fertile soil for exploration in this passage.

[4]C.K. Barrett, *A Critical and Exegetical Commentary on the Acts of the Apostles* (2 vols.; Edinburgh, UK: T. & T. Clark, 1994-1998), 771.

[5]E.g., Joseph A. Fitzmyer, *The Acts of the Apostles: A New Translation with Introduction and Commentary* (AB 31; New York. NY: Doubleday, 1998), 579.

[6]Colin J. Hemer, *The Book of Acts in the Setting of Hellenistic History* (ed. Conrad H. Gempf; WUNT 49; Tübingen: J.C.B. Mohr [Paul Siebeck], 1989), 112 (esp. 112-13 n. 29).

[7]Stephen Mitchell, "Archaeology in Asia Minor 1990-1998," *Archaeological Reports* 45 (1998-1999): 125-92 (here 138). On Troas, see Clyde E. Fant and Mitchell G. Reddish, *A Guide to Biblical Sites in Greece and Turkey* (Oxford, UK: Oxford University Press, 2003), 331-335; E. M. Blaiklock, *Cities of the New Testament* (Westwood, NJ: Fleming H. Revell Company, 1965), 35-38; Paul R. Trebilco, "Asia," 291-362 in *The Book of Acts in Its Graeco-Roman Setting* (ed. David W. J. Gill and Conrad Gempf; vol. 2 in The Book of Acts in Its First Century Setting; Grand Rapids, MI: Eerdmans, 1994), 357-59; more extensively, Peter Frisch, ed., *Die Inschriften von Ilion* (IGSK vol. 3; Bonn, Ger.: Rudolf Habelt, 1975). For other towns in the Troad, see Pliny *N.H.* 5.33.125-27.

[8]Fant and Reddish, *Sites*, 333.

estimates for the city's size, and some, estimating 100 persons per acre, thus have surmised 100,000 inhabitants. While this estimate may well be too high, Troas nonetheless was clearly a significant city.[9]

Although it bore the name Alexandria after its founding in the fourth century BCE, the emperor Augustus officially titled it Colonia Augusta Troas or Colonia Augusta Troadensium (*CIL* 3.39),[10] recalling the grandeur of its past. Troas was thus Alexandria Troas's preferred official title in this period.

Troas' Association with Troy

When an ancient audience heard of Paul's stay in Troas, they would have likely recalled earlier Troy. Although they were often confused in antiquity, the Roman colony of Troas was distinct from the site of ancient Troy (still inhabited as the town of Ilium). Colin Hemer notes that Troas could never "escape the historic and civic prestige of Ilium" to the north, "which continued to hold the primacy in a religious league of confederate cities."[11]

Educated persons recognized that Ilium, not Alexandria Troas, was the site of Homer's tales (Pliny *N.H.* 5.33.315). Ilium itself was not small, for archaeologists have observed 47 blocks of Roman Ilium, most of them 360 Roman feet north-south by 180 Roman feet east-west. Nevertheless, the ties between the two Troys were significant; for example, over two centuries earlier (c. 216 BCE), Troas sent a relief force of 4,000 that delivered Ilium from the attacking Gauls.[12]

Despite being ten to fifteen miles south-southwest from Homer's Troy,[13] the continuity between later Troas and its nearby famous past endured in popular thought.[14]   This Roman colony held the name

---

[9]Colin J. Hemer, "Alexandria Troas," *TynBul* 26 (1975): 79-112 (here 87-88).
[10]Hemer, *Acts in History*, 179.
[11]Hemer, "Alexandria Troas," 94, also noting that in the first century it appears that Ilium freely produced coins, but Troas did not. The wealthier part of the late Roman city apparently faced the Dardanelles (Mitchell, "Archaeology," 138).
[12]Hemer, "Alexandria Troas," 88 (citing Polybius 5.111.3-4).
[13]From the map in Hemer, "Alexandria Troas," 86 (plus a comment on 92), Ilium appears fewer than ten miles north of Alexandria Troas.
[14]With regard to continuity in Ilium itself: some supposed that the Palladium (Athena's image) might have remained in later Ilium, unless Diomedes and Odysseus actually succeeded in carrying it off (Appian *Hist. rom.* 12.8.53; despite the city's destruction!).

precisely to recall that past. In fact, Rome traced its founding to Trojans (especially in Virgil's *Aeneid*), and some cities in Phrygia claimed that Phrygian heroes in the Trojan War had founded them.[15] Troas would naturally evoke the same connection, especially for an audience outside the Troad. Some believed that the fallen heroes of the Trojan War still lived in the area of Troy.[16]

Greeks recognized Troy as the subject of their most famous and widely read epic, the *Iliad*,[17] and allusions to this story pervaded Greek literature.[18] Well over a millennium after the purported time of its fall, educated people at banquets might take turns reciting the final leaders of Troy (Athen. *Deipn.* 10.457F); and those who thought of Troy in their own day typically associated it with its past suffering (Athen. Deipn. 8.351a).[19] Linked with the famous past, both Alexandria Troas and Troy remained popular destinations for tourism.[20]

Given the ancient Greek association of the Troad with the Greek point of entry into Asia, Greeks familiar with the *Iliad* and the famous conquest of Asia by Alexander of Macedon (treated below) would view this as a strategic geographic point in the narrative.[21] But whereas the traditional Greek storyline was a military invasion of Asia (under Alexander's spread of Greek civilization),[22] here messengers of what would be perceived as an Asian faith take that faith westward to Europe.

---

[15]Stephen Mitchell, *Anatolia: Land, Men, and Gods in Asia Minor* (2 vols.; Oxford, UK: Clarendon, 1993), 1:208.

[16]Especially emphasized in Philostratus *Hrk.* 2.11; 11.7; 18.1-2; but the local tradition of Hector's appearances appears in Maximus of Tyre 9.7.

[17]Philostratus *Hrk.* 25.13, complains that Homer departs from this stated subject after *Il.* 22. Homer's actual explicit theme in the *Iliad* is the conflict between Agamemnon and Achilles (*Il.* 1.6-7) and how Achilles' stubborn anger led to many deaths (1.1-5).

[18]E.g., Lucian *Prof. P.S.* 20.

[19]In Dio Chrys. *Or.* 33.8, the actor apparently would have acted out Troy's fall, to the displeasure of his audience in Ilium; Troy was among the most prominent cities to fall in Lucian *Charon* 23.

[20]Detlev Dormeyer and Florencio Galindo, *Die Apostelgeschichte: Ein Kommentar für die Praxis* (Stuttgart, Ger.: Verlag Katholisches Bibelwerk, 2003), 245.

[21]Believers living in Troas itself might envision this less so, since their local experience would not be limited to their knowledge of ancient traditions.

[22]In reality, fusing Greek and Asian cultures.

The Troad, Europe, and Asia

One nuance associated with Troy was that it guarded the Hellespont, since at least Homeric times the Greek boundary between Asia and Europe (e.g., Varro 7.2.21).[23] Greeks crossed via the Hellespont into Asia (e.g., Polyb. 4.46.1), as the Persians did into Europe (Lysias Or. 2.28, §193). But whereas Greeks invaded Asia in the eras of the *Iliad* and (from Macedonia) of Alexander,[24] now the gospel comes from Asia to Greece, Macedonia, and the rest of Europe. Greek and Roman literature normally portray movements from Europe to Asia as more positive than the reverse. Jewish people, however, would think differently, as would those adopted into and committed to a Jewish movement.

Greeks and Romans viewed the legendary Trojan War as a clash between Europe and Asia.[25] Thus, for example, a Roman tragedy could have as a Trojan lament the loss of "mighty Asia's pillar."[26] For some, this war became a prototype of the continuing clash between Greek and eastern cultures.[27]

In more recent history, Greek intellectuals similarly viewed Alexander's crossing the Hellespont as marking his entrance into Asia from Europe.[28] Hence, the war between Alexander and Persia was between Europe and Asia,[29] and some alleged that Alexander struck his

---

[23]Between Macedonia and the part of the world including Syria (hence Judea), Phoenicia and Egypt in Pausanias *Geog.* 1.6.5. On western Turkey as the boundary for Asia, see e.g., Hilary Le Cornu with Joseph Shulam, *A Commentary on the Jewish Roots of Acts* (Jerusalem, Israel: Nitivyah Bible Instruction Ministry, 2003), 78.

[24]Although Demosthenes *Philip.* 3.31 complained that Macedonians were not only barbarians but even unfit as slaves, subsequent Hellenistic civilization treated both Macedonians and the Hellenized ruling class in Asia as culturally Greek.

[25]Virgil *Aen.* 7.224; Ovid *Am.* 2.12.18; Apollodorus *Epit.* 3.1; Maximus of Tyre 35.4; Menander Rhetor 2.13, 423.17-19; Philostratus the Elder *Imagines* 1.1. One could even depict the mythical flight of Jason and Medea from Colchis, from the generation preceding the Trojan War, as Europe opposing Asia (Valerius Flaccus 8.396).

[26]Seneca *Troj.* 6-7.

[27]From an ethnocentric Greek perspective (which classified the non-Hellenized as barbarians), the Trojan War was a war of Europe against barbarians (Philost. *Hrk.* 31.2). This war became the prototype of any subsequent wars between Greeks and barbarians, particularly those across the Hellespont (Philost. *Hrk.* 23.12; cf. 23.16).

[28]Polybius 3.6.4; Menander Rhetor 2.17, 444.4-5. Cf. Alexander's alleged critique of his father's ambition to cross Europe to Asia (Plutarch *Alex.* 9.5, complaining that he was too drunk even to move between couches).

[29]Quintus Curtius 4.1.38.

spear into the ground to claim Asia as his conquest (Ps-Callisth. *Alex.*
1.28). Thus, Roman observers claimed that Alexander conquered Asia
but never attempted to conquer Europe (including Italy; Livy 9.16.19)
or that the Macedonian empire controlled large parts of Europe and
most of Asia in its heyday (Livy 31.1.7).[30]

Some Greeks viewed Alexander's invasion of Asia against the
Persians as a deliberate reminiscence of Achilles's fight against Troy.
Tradition insisted that Alexander (who viewed himself as a second
Achilles) recalled this comparison, invoking the "spirit of Achilles"
against the Persians.[31]   Alexandria Troas bore Alexander's name
(although Luke omits "Alexandria"); and tradition claimed that the
city was founded in 334 BCE, which was during his lifetime.[32]

Greeks and the Romans both counted Persia as Asia,[33] Persian
attacks on Greece as Asian designs on Europe,[34] and their defeats after
invading Greece as Europe's conquest of Asia.[35] Because Greeks and
Romans often encountered Asian kingdoms in periods of the latters'
weakness, Asia sometimes received the unfair caricature[36] of cowardice
in contrast to Europe and Africa, which, they claimed, proved harder
to subdue (Appian *Hist. rom.* pref. 9).[37]   (Romans, however, knew

---

[30]Livy elsewhere couples Greece and Asia (37.53.7; 38.48.3; 38.51.3) and contrasts
Asia (esp. Asia Minor) with Europe (esp. Greece; 34.58.2-3; 37.53.13; 37.54.20).

[31] Plutarch *Alex.* 15.4; Philostratus *Hrk.* 53.16. He allegedly took a sacred shield
from the Trojan temple of Athena (Arrian *Alex.* 6.9.3).

[32]Hemer, "Alexandria Troas," 81; cf. Menander Rhetor 2.17, 444.8-9. The tradition
has been questioned; cf. F. F. Bruce, *The Acts of the Apostles: The Greek Text with
Introduction and Commentary* (Grand Rapids, MI: Eerdmans, 1951), 311; see also Pliny
N.H. 5.33.124.

[33]E.g., Aeschylus *Pers.* 73 (they ruled Asia; Greece, by contrast, is in Europe, *Pers.*
799); Aelius Aristides *Panath.* 13, 157D-158D.

[34] Lysias *Or.* 2.21, §192; 2.28, §193; Cornelius Nepos 1 (Miltiades), 3.4; 17
(Agesilaus), 2.1; Philostratus *Hrk.* 28.11.

[35]Thucydides 1.89.2 (Persians retreating from Europe); Valerius Maximus 6.9. ext.
2; Cornelius Nepos 2 (Themistocles), 5.3.

[36]Yet even Xenophon, whose *Anabasis* demonstrated Persia's military weakness
(providing groundwork for Alexander's later invasion), respected Persia's glorious past
(fictionalized in his *Cyr.*).

[37]"Barbarian Asia" opposed Greece's greater glory (Valerius Maximus 4.6. ext. 3).
The frequent exclusive prejudice for classical rather than ancient Near Eastern
foundations for modern western civilization (e.g., Max Weber, *The Agrarian Sociology of
Ancient Civilizations* [trans. R. I. Frank; London, UK: New Left Books, 1976]; see Guy
Oakes, "On Max Weber's *Agrarian Sociology of Ancient Civilizations*," *British Journal
of Sociology* 28, no. 2 [1977]: 242-43) follows too readily the classical Greek division of
the world.

better than to believe that caricature when applying it to their dreaded Parthian rivals.)[38] Yet when Gauls crossed the Hellespont to invade the Troad, Alexandria Troas' inhabitants fought back (Polyb. 5.111.1-7), which served as a good warning to Europe's barbarians not to invade Asia too eagerly (5.111.7).

Culturally, Asia Minor was increasingly Hellenized and Romanized; but symbolically, its heritage (epitomized especially by Troy and the wider ancient empire of Persia) could be treated differently. After the Hellenistic cultural revival of the second century, those who wove legends reported the enduring hatred toward Troy of the Greek hero Achilles's ghost, which was still hovering near Troy (Philost. *V.A.* 4.11; *Hrk.* 56.6-10), and the continuing Greek perception that Troy was hostile territory (Philost. *Hrk.* 53.13).[39] Scholars have argued that the location of the Protesilaos cult on the Hellespont suited that hero's role as avenger of non-Greek incursions against Greeks, guarding Europe from barbarian Asia.[40]

Between Asia and Europe?

Some doubt that we should overemphasize the division between Asia and Europe here, since the Greek language was dominant in both Macedonia and most of urban Asia Minor plus Philippi and Troas were both Roman colonies.[41] A stronger reason to doubt the distinction's relevance is that Luke does not mention it. The context applies the title "Asia" only to the Roman province in the narrowest sense (16:6), and the title "Europe" appears nowhere in the New Testament.[42]

We should also keep in mind the serious danger of understanding these categories anachronistically. For example, Asia Minor and

---

[38]See comment below.

[39] Pliny *N.H.* 5.33.125 reported an earlier monument to Achilles near his tomb in the Troad; cf. Philostratus *Vit. Apoll.* 4.11.

[40]Jennifer K. Berenson Maclean and Ellen Bradshaw Aitken, *Flavius Philostratus: Heroikos* (Atlanta, GA: Society of Biblical Literature, 2001), lix. Still, Philostratus also recognizes the continuing power of the hero Hector (*Hrk.* 19.3-7, esp. his help in 19.4 and vengeance in 19.5-7).

[41]See Ben Witherington III, *The Acts of the Apostles: A Socio-Rhetorical Commentary* (Grand Rapids, MI: Eerdmans, 1998), 486.

[42]Hemer, "Alexandria Troas," 99-100.

Greece belonged to the shared cultural sphere of the Hellenistic fusion of Greek and Asian civilizations, whereas northern Europe was entirely outside the Hellenistic cultural sphere (but not unknown to them), like China or African Meroë. In fact, northern Europe, such as Germany, was in a sense less in their sphere of valuable trade than India[43] and China,[44] although less distant and affording more direct contact.[45] Cultural spheres varied from one period to another and cannot be identified with traditional continental divisions, which simply reflect ancient Greek geographic prejudices.[46] By this period, the ancient Jewish population (central to the biblical story) spanned both the Roman and Parthian empires, thoroughly ignoring old Greek categories.

Having acknowledged these caveats, however, it remains the case that most Roman and urban eastern Mediterranean audiences would readily recognize the symbolic historic division between civilizations represented by the movement from Troas to Macedonia. Although the word "Asia" by itself in 16:6 does not imply Europe as a contrast,[47] I suspect that few members of Luke's audience who were familiar with the most prominent stories of Greek culture would fail to think of Asia and Europe when hearing of Troas and Macedonia in 16:8-9.

That Luke's culturally literate ideal audience would know such divisions is certain. Greeks divided the world into Asia (the civilizations to their east with which they had once fought bitter

---

[43]For trade connections, see e.g., Pliny *N.H.* 8.4.7-8; 9.54.106-9; 12.8.17; 12.41.84; Mortimer Wheeler, *Rome Beyond the Imperial Frontiers* (Westport, CT: Greenwood, 1971; London, UK: G. Bell & Sons, 1954), 115-71; Hans-Joachim Drexhage, "India, trade with," 6:773-777 in *Brill's New Pauly*; Lionel Casson, *The Ancient Mariners: Seafarers and Sea Fighters of the Mediterranean in Ancient Times* (2nd ed.; Princeton, NJ: Princeton University Press, 1991), 199, 204-6; for religious and philosophic connections, e.g., Juvenal *Sat.* 6.585; Philostratus *Vit. Apoll.* Bks. 2-3; for political connections, e.g., Suetonius *Aug.* 21.3. For a fuller treatment, see comment on Acts 1:8 in Keener, [*Acts: An Exegetical Commentary*, vol. 1].

[44]E.g., Pliny *N.H.* 12.1.2; 12.41.84; Casson, *Mariners*, 198, 205-6; Lin Ying, "Ruler of the Treasure Country: the Image of the Roman Empire in Chinese Society from the First to the Fourth Century AD," *Latomus* 63, no. 2 (2004): 327-39; Kevin Herbert, "The Silk Road: The Link between the Classical World and Ancient China," *Classical Bulletin* 73, no. 2 (1997): 119-24.

[45]Traders with the Roman empire reached even Annam (today's Vietnam) by the late 2nd century, and others "traded with Malaya and Java" (Casson, *Mariners*, 205).

[46]For the danger of mixing apples and oranges by confusing cultural spheres with traditional Greek continental divisions, cf. Usry and Keener, *Black Man's Religion*, 41-44.

[47]"Asia" in 16:6 is the Roman province, not Greater Asia.

conflicts), Europe, and often Africa (on the south of the Mediterranean sea)—a distinction that continued in later literature.[48] Some Greeks even divided the world into just Asia and Europe by including Africa in Europe.[49]

Because of the subjects addressed by most writers, the division between Europe and Asia proved to be the essential one in most texts.[50] Some treated this distinction as if it were as pervasive as that between Greek and barbarian (e.g., Ps.-Dion. Hal. *Epid.* 3.268) or between heaven and earth (Varro 5.5.31). The distinction was geographic (purely in terms of historic perceptions), not cultural. Thus, Asia included the cities that were traditionally Athenian colonies in Asia Minor, although Greece was part of Europe.[51] Even more clearly, audiences in the Roman Empire would regard Judea as part of Asia.

Romans, like Greeks, expressed both grudging respect for Asia (notably Parthia,[52] but also some great civilizations beyond)[53] and irrational xenophobia (such as Juvenal's oft-noted comparison of eastern "cults" like Judaism with the refuse of the Syrian river Orontes).[54] As one source points out, Romans expressed their own "Eurocentric chauvinism", such as when Pliny the Elder calls Europe "conqueror of the earth" and "by far the loveliest portion of the earth" (*N.H.* 3.1.5).[55] Since they claimed descent from Troy, however, they owed some respect to their own Asian heritage.

---

[48]E.g., Cicero *Rosc. Amer.* 31.103; Sallust *Jug.* 17.3; Pliny *N.H.* 3.1.3; Dio Chrysostom *Or.* 4.49.

[49]A view of some geographers noted in Sallust *Jug.* 17.3 (who treats Egypt as part of Asia, 17.4). The world's primary division in Philo *Mos.* 2.20 is Europe and Asia, although he writes from Alexandria. Some texts mention just the two, but perhaps because only these two are relevant to their point (e.g., Dio Chrysostom *Or.* 8.29). On the background and ancient understandings of the Europe/Asia distinction, cf. also Eckart Olshausen, "Europe/Europa," 5:206-210 in *Brill's New Paully*, especially 209.

[50]E.g., Aeschines *Ctes.* 250; Thucydides 2.97.6; Manetho *Aeg.* frg. 35.3; Livy 34.58.2-3; Appian *Hist. rom.* 11.9.56; 11.10.63; *Bell. civ.* 4.17.134; Menander Rhetor 2.10, 417.13-17 (on excellent governors in both, esp. 417.14).

[51]E.g., Appian *Hist. rom.* 11.2.6. Asia Minor was only a small part of greater Asia, which included, e.g., Scythia (Ptolemy *Tetrab.* 2.3.60).

[52]See e.g., Pliny *N.H.* 6.29.112—6.31.141. Still, Parthians were called barbarians (e.g., Dio Chrysostom *Or.* 72.3; Josephus *Ant.* 14.343; *War* 1.264).

[53]See comments on India and China above.

[54]Juvenal *Sat.* 3.62.

[55]LCL 2:5; see also Eric Herbert Warmington and Simon Hornblower, "Europe," 574 in *OCD*. Pliny viewed Europe as only a bit smaller than Asia and Africa combined in *N.H.* 6.38.210, and as roughly half the world in 3.1.5.

Asia's Gift to Europe

Luke cannot readily share the above-mentioned prejudices of some of his Greek and Roman contemporaries, because the faith he recounts would be viewed by his audience as "Asian."[56] Whatever his own geographic location, the early Christian movement to which he belongs was numerically stronger in Asia than in Europe. Luke-Acts reports the story of Jesus in Asia, uses Septuagintal Greek, and otherwise would appear to Hellenistic historiographers as Asian historiography (just as Josephus did).[57]

Thus in a sense, Acts narrates the beginning of what some could have viewed as an Asian movement's (spiritual) conquest in the reverse direction. Jews were considered Asian; and the gospel coming from Asia to Europe reversed the Greek invasions of Troy and, more recently, Alexander's invasion of Persia.[58] But Asia's gift of the gospel to Europe was better in this case than Hellenization or Roman conquest—although many traditional Greeks and Romans would demur. Rome had made peace with Hellenization, but a writer there could (as we have noted) compare eastern cults to Syrian refuse pouring into the Tiber (Juvenal Sat. 3.62). At the same time, those who lashed out against "eastern customs" in Rome often did so precisely in reaction against other Romans who embraced such customs.[59]

---

[56]Of course the salvation-historical issue was specifically Jewish (a gift to all Gentiles, Rom 15:27); my point is only that, by traditional Greek categories known and used by Luke's audience, Judea belonged to Asia.

[57]See David L. Balch, "METABOLH POLITEIWN—Jesus as Founder of the Church in Luke-Acts: Form and Function," 139-88 in *Contextualizing Acts: Lukan Narrative and Greco-Roman Discourse* (ed. Todd Penner and Caroline Vander Stichele; SBLSymS 20; Atlanta, GA: Society of Biblical Literature, 2003), 152-53, 186. It was not without reason that, in the heyday of historians wrongly calling mystery cults "oriental," Harvard classicist Arthur Darby Nock pointed out that Christianity was more Oriental in character than the mysteries ("The Vocabulary of the New Testament," *JBL* 52 [1933]: 131-39, here 136).

[58]It was also more successful than the failed Persian invasion under Xerxes. It was not, of course, a military invasion, but a sort of cultural infiltration, an approach more successful in the past. (Hellenistic culture, although maintaining Greek as its dominant element, involved significant cultural fusion.).

[59]Regarding Judaism, see John G. Gager, *The Origins of Anti-Semitism: Attitudes Toward Judaism in Pagan and Christian Antiquity* (New York, NY: Oxford, 1983), 55-56; Zvi Yavetz, "Judeophobia in Classical Antiquity: A Different Approach," *JJS* 44, no. 1 (1993): 1-22. Many in the Greco-Roman world were attracted to what they regarded as the exotic and esoteric lore of the east or Egypt (e.g., Valerius Maximus 8.7. ext. 2-3; Lucian *Cock* 18; *Phil. Sale* 3; Iamblichus *V.P.* 3.14; 4.19).

That Paul and Silas voyage in 16:10-12 from Troas to Macedonia reinforces the possibility that some of Luke's audience might hear a contrast with Alexander, the Macedonian who invaded Asia at Troy (see comment above). Of course, people sailed from Troas to Macedonia and vice versa on a regular basis (e.g., Acts 20:5-6), but in view of continental boundaries that most envisioned, this juncture in Luke's narrative appears significant.

Luke's first volume is framed by scenes in Jerusalem's temple (Luke 1:5-22; 24:52-53), but his second volume is driven by the movement from Jerusalem (Acts 1 through 7) to Rome (28:16-31). The voyage from the Roman colony of Troas to Macedonia would bring them to the Via Egnatia, a Roman road that constituted a major link between Italy and Asia Minor in the Roman period.[60] Many scholars believe that, by starting on the Via Egnatia, Paul was already signaling his interest in Rome,[61] although conflict in Thessalonica may have turned him southward.

Moreover, from Luke's salvation-historical perspective, the gospel's spread was even more significant for history than Alexander's conquests and cultural fusion. Passing from Troas to Macedonia here is thus no mere customary voyage. Given the movement of the narrative as a whole and the epic dimension of that movement, this transition might evoke Alexander in reverse. It probably evokes at least the traditional divide between continents, showing that this Asian faith can reach all cultures.

If one resists all of these conclusions by pointing out that Luke does not explicitly mention this division, one might infer that he does not regard continental divisions as significant. At the very least, however, it is certain that many Gentiles who heard Acts would have heard the narrative's movement the way they understood other movements from Asia (whether the cult of Cybele or Judaism)—as that of an Asian faith establishing itself in Europe.

---

[60]Nigel G. L. Hammond, "The Western Part of the Via Egnatia," *JRS* 64 (1974): 185-94; cf. Ludwig Friedländer, *Roman Life and Manners Under the Early Empire* (4 vols.; trans. L. A. Magnus et al.; New York, NY: Barnes & Noble, 1907-1913), 1:284.

[61]E.g., Günther Bornkamm, *Early Christian Experience* (trans. Paul L. Hammer; New York, NY: Harper & Row; London: SCM, 1969), 15.

Conclusion

A first-century audience in the Roman Empire would recognize in Acts 16:8-10 the call of Asian believers to spread Jesus's message into Europe. Luke's larger narrative includes all three continents, noting the initial foray of the gospel into Africa (Acts 8:26-40, recounting the first Gentile Christian)[62] and later into Europe toward the heart of the Roman Empire. Luke's audience would not await a signal of the gospel's movement to Asia, however, because his original audience recognized the place of its beginnings (that dominate all of Luke's first volume and a substantial part of his second volume) as being in Asia.

Not all of my suggestions in this article are of equal weight. That Luke's audience understood Jesus's movement and the apostolic mission as beginning in Asia is certain. That Luke envisioned the movement from Troas to Macedonia as a transition from Asia to Europe I regard as very likely. (Although because he is not more explicit, I can be less certain how much he makes of this.) Lastly, I believe it possible—and even fairly likely—that much of his audience could hear a reversal of Alexander's Macedonian invasion of Asia in this narrative. Because he does not evoke that history more clearly (in contrast to his often explicit biblical allusions), it is uncertain to what degree Luke himself intended such an allusion. Nevertheless, ancient narratives evoked such history frequently enough to suggest the plausibility of this final point and to invite further exploration by some scholars interested in that question. At the very least, we can be confident that many of Luke's ancient hearers would have envisioned such connections.

---

[62] See Craig S. Keener, "Novels' 'Exotic' Places and Luke's African Official (Acts 8:27)," *Andrews University Seminary Studies* 46, no. 1 (2008): 5-20; for the subsequent spread of the gospel in Africa, cf. also Craig S. Keener, "The Aftermath of the Ethiopian Eunuch," *A.M.E. Church Review* 118, no. 385 (2002): 112-24.

APTS PRESS
ASIAN JOURNAL
& OF PENTECOSTAL
STUDIES

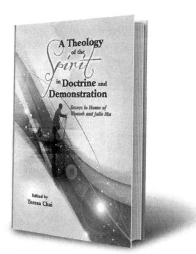

A Theology of the Spirit in Doctrine and Demonstration:
Essays in Honor of Wonsuk and Julie Ma
Editor: Teresa Chai

Theology in Context: A Case Study in the Philippines
Dave Johnson

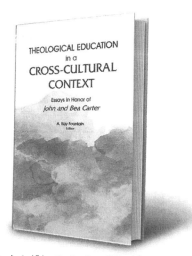

Theological Education in a Cross-Cultural Context:
Essays in Honor of John and Bea Carter
Editor: A. Kay Fountain

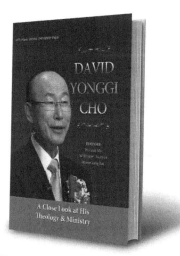

David Yonggi Cho: A Close Look at His Theology & Ministry
Editors: William W. Menzies, Wonsuk Ma and
Hyeon-sung Bae

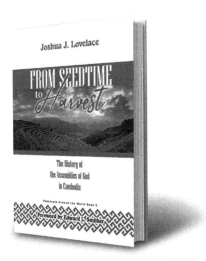
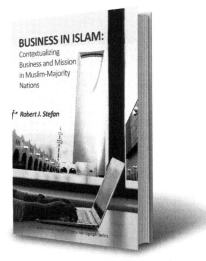

Seedtime to Harvest: The History of the Assemblies of God
in Cambodia
Joshua Lovelace

Business in Islam: Contextualizing Business and
Mission in Muslim-Majority Nations
Robert Stefan

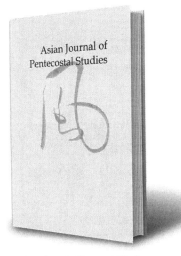

To the Ends of the Earth: Building a National
Missionary Sending Structure
Arto Hämäläinen and Ulf Strohbehn

Asian Journal of Pentecostal Studies

APTS PRESS
& ASIAN JOURNAL OF PENTECOSTAL STUDIES

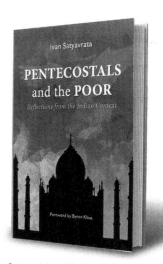

Pentecostals and the Poor: Reflections From
the Indian Context
Ivan Satyavrata

A Theology of Hope: Contextual Perspectives
in Korean Pentecostalism
Sang Yun Lee

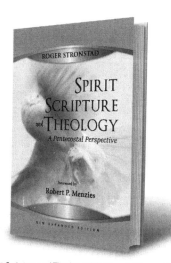

Spirit Scripture and Theology: A Pentecostal Perspective
Robert Stronstad

Training Asian to Reach The World: Essays Honoring
Everett and Evelyn McKinney for 50 Years in Missions
Dave Johnson

APTS PRESS
ASIAN JOURNAL
& OF PENTECOSTAL
STUDIES

Leave a Legacy: Increasing Missionary Longevity
Russ Turney

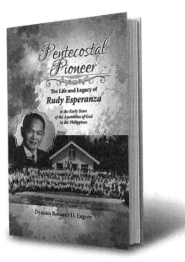

Pentecostal Pioneer: The Life and Legacy of Rudy Esperanza in the
Early Years of the Assemblies of God in the Philippines
Dynnice Rosanny D. Engcoy

The Old Testament in Theology and Teaching:
Essays in Honor of Kay Fountain
Editors: Teresa Chai and Dave Johnson

Understanding the Iglesia ni Cristo: What They Really Believe
and How They Can Be Reached
Anne C. Harper